SUSHI
with Style

ELLEN BROWN

photography by THERESA RAFFETTO

STERLING

New York / London
www.sterlingpublishing.com

STERLING and the distinctive Sterling logo are
registered trademarks of Sterling Publishing Co., Inc.

Library of Congress Cataloging-in-Publication Data Available

2   4   6   8   10   9   7   5   3   1

Published by Sterling Publishing Co., Inc.
387 Park Avenue South, New York, NY 10016
© 2008 by Ellen Brown
Photography © 2008 by Theresa Raffetto
Distributed in Canada by Sterling Publishing
c/o Canadian Manda Group, 165 Dufferin Street
Toronto, Ontario, Canada M6K 3H6
Distributed in the United Kingdom by GMC Distribution Services
Castle Place, 166 High Street, Lewes, East Sussex, England BN7 1XU
Distributed in Australia by Capricorn Link (Australia) Pty. Ltd.
P.O. Box 704, Windsor, NSW 2756, Australia

Design by Stewart A. Williams
Interior illustrations by Kate Quinby
Food Stylist: Tara Bench
Food Stylist and Consultant: Mamie Nishide
Prop Stylist: Lorie Reilly

Printed in China
All rights reserved

Sterling ISBN-13: 978-1-4027-5572-9
ISBN-10: 1-4027-5572-4

For information about custom editions, special sales, premium and
corporate purchases, please contact Sterling Special Sales
Department at 800-805-5489 or specialsales@sterlingpublishing.com.

CONTENTS

Acknowledgments

Writing a book is a solitary endeavor, but its publication is always a team effort. My thanks go to . . .

Carlo DeVito and Pamela Horn of Sterling Publishing for their vision and guidance.

Christine Legon, Melissa Gerber, and Megan Rotondo of Sterling Publishing for their editing and production expertise.

Theresa Raffetto, whose luscious photography so enlivens these pages.

Tara Bench, food stylist extraordinaire, and Mamie Nishide, who provided the authenticity for the way dishes are presented. Also to prop stylist Lorie Reilly for her role in accessorizing these exquisite photographs.

Ed Claflin, my agent, for his unfailing support and humor.

Tigger-Cat Brown and Patches-Kitten Brown, my furry companions, who were thrilled with all the fish scraps that ended up in their food bowls.

Preface

DURING A RECENT WEB SEARCH I found sushi restaurants garnering rave reviews in such non-Asian centers as Billings, Montana, and Birmingham, Alabama; sushi is being delivered in Buenos Aires, Argentina, too. Then I came across an article in *The New York Times* about a group of young professionals in Iowa coming together for a sushi-making party in lieu of a summer barbecue, and I found literally hundreds of ongoing blogs for anyone wanting guidance on making sushi at home.

I have little doubt that sushi will become the pizza of the new millennium. It meets all the criteria necessary to leave the realm of trendy foods and become part of the mainstream of our country's culinary repertoire:

It is easy to make, and requires almost no specialized equipment;
the few cooking skills necessary are easy to master;
it is open to endless variation and personalization; and
it is relatively inexpensive.

As evidence that this process is already in motion, take a look at the take-out food cases of America's mainstream supermarkets—not specialty markets deemed "gourmet." You'll find freshly made "supermarket sushi" and, frequently, a sushi chef behind the counter making the rolls to order. You'll also find sushi on the menu at sports stadiums, and in the food courts of the country's suburban shopping malls. In fact, sushi is passed as an hors d'oeuvre at cocktail parties and weddings.

And why not? There are many reasons why sushi appeals to today's health-conscious nation: It's low in fat and high in protein. Oily fish such as salmon and tuna are high in omega-3 fatty acids, which are viewed as important to prevent heart disease, and most fish is also high in vitamin B_{12}, which is essential for building cells. And condiments such as wasabi, pickled ginger, and soy sauce all contain antibacterial properties.

Another aspect of eating sushi that makes it healthful is that it is eaten slowly; it's chewy and needs to be chewed well. This slower eating triggers a reaction in the stomach that tells you you're full. And part of the prolonged eating process is just reveling in how beautifully the food is presented; we eat first with our eyes. Even in the refrigerated case at a supermarket, the presentation is stunning; and you can hardly find anything similar in an American fast food restaurant!

If you are new to the sushi experience and somewhat squeamish about the concept of raw fish, then start with the vegetarian items and dishes made with cooked seafood such as the California roll; other options are sushi made with shrimp or barbecued eel. Many sushi restaurants serve tempura items tucked inside rolls; those are always cooked as well. If you want to avoid the sight of a slice of raw fish staring at you on the plate, then select a *maki* roll of some type with the fish as a small section tucked into the center rather than a piece of *nigiri-zushi,* which will have it displayed prominently on top.

When you are ready to move on, start with the raw versions of fish you already like when they are cooked. For example, if you like smoked salmon and grilled salmon, then chances are you will like raw salmon. Another way to begin is with fish that are mildly flavored, such as sea scallops or halibut. A general rule is that the less oily a fish, the less "fishy" it will taste.

But many listings on today's sushi menus are far from authentic. As was the case with pizza, sushi is undergoing a transformation, and you'll find both traditional and contemporary recipes in this book. In the same way that innovative chefs like Wolfgang Puck topped pizza with smoked salmon and caviar in place of sausage and cheese, many chefs around the country today are using the rolled form of a *maki* to encase strips of grilled beef flavored with Mexican spices. This process began decades ago with the American invention of the California roll—not part and parcel of all sushi menus, though its presence is growing in this century.

And that is part of the fun of *Sushi with Style*. Once you've mastered the very easy basics of making sushi rice and learning to roll with a bamboo mat, then the sky is the limit!

Ellen Brown
Providence, Rhode Island

ontrary to many preconceptions, sushi has nothing to do with fish. It is all about the rice and literally means "vinegared rice." As you will read in the history below, sushi developed from the ancient technique of preserving fish by fermenting it in cooked rice, and the rice is all-important to the quality of sushi—regardless of whether you eat it in a restaurant or produce it in your kitchen. And you will be pleased to learn that creating the perfectly seasoned and perfectly textured rice for sushi can be accomplished in a matter of minutes.

Sushi with Style intends to demystify sushi, so that you will feel comfortable making it in your own home. Many different types of sushi are introduced by their proper names and common names; in the proper names, "sushi" changes to "zushi" when used as a modifier for a particular form. In the upcoming chapters you will learn everything there is to know to successfully make these simple and healthful treats.

Sushi's History

COMPARED WITH OTHER ASPECTS OF JAPANESE CULTURE, sushi as we know it today is a new kid on the block; it was developed in the nineteenth century. But its roots reach back to the fourth century BCE and the Mekong River area of Southeast Asia. In these inland areas, the seasonal flooding of the rice paddies would bring fish with the water, and the farmers developed a crude form of aquaculture.

It was then and there that fish was first fermented in cooked rice as a method of food preservation, but the rice was then discarded because it smelled so awful. This dish, which served as a prototype for sushi, was mentioned in Chinese dictionaries by the second century CE, and it was introduced to Japan in the seventh century.

During the Muromachi period of Japanese history (1336–1573) the Japanese began to eat the rice along with the fish, but the first innovation we can tie to contemporary sushi occurred in the seventeenth century. It was then that Matsumoto Yoshiichi, a doctor in Tokyo (then called Edo) employed by Ietsuna, the fourth Tokugawa shogun, began mixing rice vinegar with the rice to give it a better flavor. But it was still not eaten right away. It was placed in a press similar to those used today to make *oshi-zushi*, and it stood for at least a few days to pickle. The sushi chef's workstation today is still called *tsube-ba*, which means "pickling place."

It took more than a century to move closer to our sushi of today, and that transformation also took place in Edo in 1824, where sushi had become fast food; it was sold from stalls along the street. One enterprising stall owner in the city's Ryogoku district, Hanaya Yohei, began topping vinegar-laced rice with pieces of fresh fish caught in the waters of Edo Bay, thus creating the ancestor of today's *nigiri-zushi*. It was at this time that the custom of serving sushi in pairs began. Originally it was served as one large piece, but when customers preferred it cut in half, that became the custom.

The sushi stalls were set on wheels and were hauled into place each evening. Without access to running water, the chefs had to fill buckets from obliging residents in nearby houses. Their fish selection was kept chilled in a box filled with ice, and they would lift its bamboo cover to display the evening's options to potential patrons.

The sushi rice was cooked at home and kept behind the counter; during cold months it would be wrapped in straw to keep it from becoming too chilled to be pliable. On the small counter for the patrons were communal bowls of soy sauce (*shoyu*) and pickled ginger (*gari*).

When they were ready to open up for the evening, they would hang out their *noren* curtain, a colorful printed cloth used in homes as a room divider; it was used as a communal napkin by patrons. The eating process was improved later in the century when sheets of *nori* were wrapped around the rice similar to today's *temaki* (hand rolls) to keep fingers from getting overly sticky.

By the end of the nineteenth century, sushi in Edo was an established part of the bustling city's culinary culture. It was delivered to both offices and homes, and it was taken along on flower-viewing excursions, a popular form of entertainment. Some famous Japanese woodblock prints from the late nineteenth century depict the subject.

While sushi was in vogue in Edo, it was virtually unknown in most parts of Japan until after the Great Kanto Earthquake of 1923. As a result of the devastation, the chefs lost their customer base, so they moved around to other parts of Japan—and introduced sushi. After World War II, the stalls were closed by the American forces, so sushi chefs moved to indoor spaces.

In the same way that returning GIs brought tales of gooey pizza from the beaches of Italy and flaky croissants from the cities of France, they also brought home memories of sushi from Japan.

However, America's romance with sushi began only about forty years ago. Sushi arrived in the United States via Los Angeles's Little Tokyo in the 1960s. It was introduced by a man named Noritoshi Kanai, who worked for Mutual Trading Company and previously had tried to introduce snake meat and chocolate-covered ants to the United States as he looked for products to sell to Americans. Sushi was slow to catch on beyond the Japanese community for more than a decade, appealing primarily to businessmen who frequently visited Japan.

This all changed with the invention of the clearly nonauthentic California roll in the early 1970s. Most food historians credit Ichiro Mashita, sushi chef at Tokyo Kaikan restaurant in Los Angeles, as its father because he noticed the similarity of texture of avocado and tuna (*toro*). His substitution created the prototype for a dish accessible to millions of Americans who previously shied away from the concept of eating raw fish.

Sushi has progressed from being an exotic and adventurous novelty to being offered everywhere; there are now an estimated nine thousand sushi restaurants in the United States alone, with countless thousands of other retail outlets in supermarkets. As an indication of its increasing popularity, just one outlet of New York's famous Monster Sushi chain served more than seven tons of tuna alone in 2004. And as you make the simple recipes in this book, you'll add your kitchen to the list of venues.

two SUSHI BASICS

R egardless of cuisine, the basic recipe for success in cooking is to have the right equipment and ingredients, and to have the skills to know how to handle both. That is the information you will find in this chapter.

Equipment

ONE OF THE REASONS THAT IT IS SO EASY to make sushi at home is because with few exceptions you probably already have everything you need. If you get hooked on the process, you may want to expand your *batterie de cuisine* to include some specialized items, like molds or a dedicated rice bowl, but it is not necessary at first, or at all for that matter.

Here's a list of kitchen basics that you probably already have or, if you do not, you should buy them because they're useful for all types of cooking:

Liquid and dry measuring cups
Measuring spoons
Cutting boards
Vegetable peeler
Fine-mesh strainer or colander
Four-sided box grater (or Japanese mandoline)
Sharp knives
Frying pan, preferably about 12 inches wide
Plastic wrap
A few large mixing bowls
Bamboo skewers
Tweezers

And here's a list of sushi-specific equipment and alternatives:

A pot in which to cook the rice. While I detail the merits of an electric rice cooker on page 18, any sturdy pot with a tight-fitting cover that doesn't allow steam to escape can be used. Another option is a slow cooker; details on how to use that item for sushi-making are also on page 18.

A bowl in which to mix the rice. The traditional Japanese wooden bowl, called a *hangiri,* is excellent because it allows the rice to cool quickly and absorbs excess moisture. The same can be said for a wooden salad bowl that's not varnished. If you have neither, rather than using a mixing bowl I suggest using a wide saucepan (preferably nonstick) or a baking pan; the dimensions of width to height are similar.

If you're using a *hangiri,* it needs to be seasoned before its first use by soaking it overnight in a large pot of water into which ¼ cup of rice vinegar per 1 quart of water has been added. Each time you use it, fill it to the brim with hot water while your rice is cooking, and then drain and dry it just before adding the rice. And as is the case for all wooden bowls, it should never be placed in the dishwasher.

A paddle with which to stir the rice. If you're going to buy one or two inexpensive pieces of equipment, this would be one of them. Called a *shamoji*, the paddle cools the rice and mixes in the ingredients without breaking the grains. Thin and wide wooden spoons or a rubber spatula are your alternatives.

Even if you make sushi only occasionally, whatever utensil you use to stir the rice should be dedicated to that job. Sushi rice has a delicate flavor, and assertive flavors that might have crept into your wooden spoons from stirring onions and garlic would not make a good addition.

Something with which to cool the rice. In traditional Japanese homes the task of fanning the rice to cool it is done by a stiff, flat fan called an *uchiwa*. However, to save time I use a small electric clip-on fan aimed at the bowl. You can also use a magazine or folded newspaper.

Lint-free kitchen towels to cover the rice. Once the rice is finished, you cover it with damp towels, called *fukin*, to keep it from drying out. You do not want to use fluffy terry-cloth because some of the threads could easily enter the rice, so use what we call tea towels—which have a flat weave—or an old pillowcase or a double layer of any cotton fabric.

Cooking chopsticks for making omelets. Called *ryoribashi*, these chopsticks are about three to four times the length of the ones with which you eat. They allow you to manipulate food with one hand, and once you've gotten accustomed to using them you'll find them indispensable for all cooking, regardless of cuisine.

A bamboo mat for rolling *maki*. This is one investment you'll want to make, and these mats cost just a few dollars. Called a *makisu*, the mat is sturdy and has slats about ⅙ to ⅛ inch wide. Most are a 9½-inch square, which is the perfect size for prepackaged sheets of *nori*.

After using the mat, wash it in warm soapy water, and allow it to dry on its side. After the cotton strings are dry, store it flat wrapped in paper towels.

The last category of equipment will only be needed if you become an aficionado and want to make a large range of styles of sushi:

Molds for making *nigiri-zushi* and *oshi-zushi*. While a professional sushi chef is unlikely to use a plastic mold to form the little fingers of rice for *nigiri-zushi*, I find these inexpensive items about as easy to use as an ice cube tray, and especially helpful when making lots of sushi for a party. But even chefs will use wooden molds to make those perfect cubes, and they are relatively expensive. I'll give you some alternatives for improvising on page 31.

A square omelet pan for making the traditional sweet egg omelet (*tamago*). You'll find there are very few circular forms involved in making sushi, and while you can use any skillet to roll this sweetened egg omelet, you will not have any waste if you use a special pan, called a *makiyakinabe*. Otherwise, trim the omelet to a square, and enjoy the trimmings as a treat.

Ingredients

SUSHI IS A REFLECTION OF JAPANESE CULTURE and its harmony with nature. While the presentation is artistic, the basic ingredients—rice, fish or other protein, and vegetables—are very simple with clean flavors. Unlike in Western cooking, with its panoply of herbs and spices, you need few ingredients in your sushi pantry for success.

But those few ingredients are very important and are used on a regular basis. This section of *Sushi with Style* introduces you to the basics. If you have problems locating some of them, consult the Mail-Order Sources on page 78.

Picking Your Fish

THE FRESHNESS AND PURITY OF THE RAW FISH used for sushi is paramount in importance for health as well as for aesthetics. You cannot walk into just any fish store and select a piece out of the case to slice and eat raw; the fish must be what is called "sushi quality," and, unfortunately, that is not easy to find.

First of all, get over any prejudice you might have against frozen food; the Food and Drug Administration mandates that all fish that is eaten raw—including for sushi or tartare—must be frozen first to kill potential parasites. The only exception is tuna, which is exceptionally clean, although much of it is frozen, too, because of its high demand on a continual basis.

To make raw saltwater fish—and freshwater fish is *never* eaten raw because of its high potential for parasites—ready for sushi it must be frozen for at least a week at a temperature of -4°F, or it can be flash-frozen for fifteen hours to a temperature of -31°F. While there is no regulation regarding the other qualities of what makes fish sushi grade, there are aesthetic considerations, such as fat content and firmness.

Restaurants have suppliers who specialize in fish for sushi, but home cooks are not as lucky. At your fish store, ask specifically about sushi-grade fish, and if you have a difficult time finding it, consult some of the Mail-Order Sources listed on page 78.

Pantry Items

WHEN YOU KEEP IN MIND THAT SUSHI DEVELOPED in an era prior to refrigeration, then it makes sense that the essential ingredients are all shelf stable; most are preserved by dehydration. Here is the list of essentials:

Rice: It is becoming easier to find the proper rice in supermarkets as well as Asian markets, where it is frequently labeled "sushi rice" to ease the selection. This species has short grains and the right balance of starches (amylose and amylopectin), which allow the rice to stick together and keep the sushi from falling apart on the trip from the plate to the mouth. *Koshihikari* and *akita komachi* are two premium quality varieties.

Nori: Next to rice, these sheets of seaweed (7 by 8 inches) are the most essential part of sushi; they form the traditional wrapper for all *maki* rolls. Once opened they should be used up quickly; they absorb humidity rapidly.

Wasabi **powder:** While you can purchase tubes of premixed *wasabi,* the fiery green Japanese horseradish used to flavor sushi, I find that mixing it yourself from powder produces a product with better flavor and aroma. Prepare only a small amount at a time; its flavor diminishes rapidly.

Rice vinegar (*su*): This mildly flavored vinegar has no substitute, but it is easy to find in the supermarket; sometimes it is shelved with other vinegars and sometimes with other Asian ingredients. Be careful to buy a vinegar that has not already been seasoned; all the recipes in this book are formulated for plain vinegar.

Soy sauce (*shoyu*): Made from fermented soybeans, this dark and salty condiment is used both as an ingredient in sushi and as a dipping sauce. Specially formulated Japanese soy sauces are available; I prefer the low-sodium types.

Pickled ginger (*gari*): Eaten to cleanse the palate between pieces of sushi, the supple slices of ginger are salted and then cooked in sweetened vinegar. Jars are available in supermarkets.

Sweet rice wine (*mirin*): This sweetened rice wine is used in many recipes, and it is easy to find. If you do not have *mirin,* add 1 teaspoon of sugar to 1 tablespoon *sake* to replicate the flavor.

Rice wine (*sake*): This stalwart of traditional Japanese beverages is used in cooking as well as enjoyed at the table.

Kelp (*kombu*): These thick, leathery sheets of sea vegetable are used to flavor *dashi,* the basic Japanese cooking stock. They are coated with a white powder, which should be wiped off before using, but do not rinse kelp or the flavor will be diminished.

Bonito flakes (*katsuo-boshi*): These flakes, made from dried and fermented fish, in addition to kelp, are necessary for making *dashi.*

Soybean paste (*miso*): This paste, made from fermented soybeans, comes both in a mild, light-colored version, and a dark red version that is more assertive and salty.

Sesame seeds (*goma*): You can find pretoasted white sesame seeds in many Asian markets, or you can toast them yourself; follow the method on page 25. Or you can use black sesame seeds, which need no toasting.

Green tea (*ocha*, but called *agari* when served with sushi): The two types you will find in markets are *bancha*, which should steep for 2 to 3 minutes, and *sencha*, which steeps for only 1 minute.

Granulated sugar: It may strike you as mundane, but granulated sugar is an essential component of the mixture that seasons sushi rice.

Refrigerated *or* Frozen Foods

FROZEN FOOD DOES NOT IMPLY that these are convenience products; they are specialty foods carried by suppliers, and some are easier to find than others.

Eel (*unagi*): First steamed, and then broiled with a glaze, barbecued eel is a staple for sushi making. It can be found in the freezer section of Asian markets, or by mail order.

Imitation crab sticks (*kani kama*): You'll find them in every supermarket; some brands clearly have better flavor than others. There is no question, though, that they make it easy to roll a *maki* because they are straight!

Eggs: I call for large eggs in all recipes in this book.

Tofu: Cubes of firm tofu are traditionally added to soups, and can become part of scattered sushi (*chirashi-zushi*).

Deep-fried tofu packets (*abura-age*): These are sold frozen, and stuffing them with seasoned rice and other ingredients is an alternative form of sushi called *inari-zushi*.

Vegetables

WHEN SHOPPING FOR VEGETABLES FOR SUSHI, always find the best quality available, and buy organic produce if possible. The vegetables are used either raw or quickly blanched, so their quality will show through.

Asparagus: While asparagus is not traditional, it is used today in many preparations. Buy the thinnest spears you can find; if they are thick, cut them into lengthwise strips after blanching.

Avocado: The small Haas avocado is the best choice for sushi, and it is essential that the avocado is ripe.

Carrots: Carrots are used as shreds, slices, and thin strips, both raw and blanched.

Chives: This herb adds its delicate onion flavor as it serves as a tie for toppings on *nigiri-zushi* and to close omelet purses. Chopped chives can also be used as a garnish.

Cucumber: Unless you have to buy a conventional cucumber that has been waxed, do not peel cucumbers for sushi; the green skin adds both color and nutrients. Small and thin Japanese cucumbers are best, followed by Kirby cucumbers (which are frequently sold as "pickling cucumbers"). An English—or hothouse—cucumber is next on the scale, and one is equal in size to four Japanese cucumbers.

Daikon: This large white Japanese radish should be peeled deeply to remove both the skin and fibers beneath it. It is used shredded, sliced, and as long strips. It is rarely, if ever, blanched.

Eggplant: The bright amethyst-toned Japanese eggplants need no salting because they are not bitter. If using a globe eggplant, peel the skin.

Green beans: Like asparagus, green beans are always blanched before being included in rolls.

Lotus root (*renkon*): There are few vegetables as attractive as slices of lotus root; they look like a flower. Like apples, they discolor easily, so drop slices immediately into a bowl of acidulated water before cooking them.

Perilla (*shiso*): This aromatic member of the mint family has a bitter flavor like that of mustard greens. The leaves, with their attractive shape and saw-toothed edges, are frequently included in bowls and plates of scattered sushi (*chirashi-zushi*).

Scallions: In most sushi it is the green leaves rather than the white bulb that are used, and they add a bright onion flavor without being overwhelming. The bulbs can be turned into brushes to use as a garnish.

Snow peas: Depending on their thickness, blanched snow peas can either be used whole in rolls or cut into thinner strips.

Sprouts: Sprouts, from peppery radish to delicate mung bean, can be used in sushi. Using them saves time; they do not need any cutting or dicing.

Wild mushrooms: While tiny delicate *enoki* mushrooms are used as a garnish either raw or lightly sautéed, more woodsy shiitake mushrooms are always cooked.

Techniques

JUST AS YOU DON'T NEED TO ADD MANY of pieces of equipment to your kitchen to make sushi, the skills required are limited; you do not have to learn how to make spun sugar swans or towers from flaky puff pastry. The two techniques that are fundamental to great sushi are making the base rice and knowing how to cut fish properly. Both of those techniques, plus a few other pointers, are presented here.

When you read about the various ways to prepare ingredients, you will notice that there is one leitmotif—ingredients are prepared so that they are in rectangular form. For example, there are tricks for cooking shrimp to remove the natural curvature and cutting cucumbers to make them into a log shape.

The All-Important Rice

BECAUSE YOU NOW KNOW THAT SUSHI MEANS vinegared rice, and about 80 percent of what you eat at a sushi meal is the rice, it should not surprise you that making that rice is of paramount importance. Anyone can boil rice and water, but to create seasoned rice with the proper flavor and texture is a bit more complicated—but not much more complicated.

You start with the right type of rice (see page 14), cook it properly, and handle it gently during the seasoning process. Your goal is to create rice with a chewy texture that is bright white and fragrant and that is sticky and moist but not wet.

The first step is to rinse the rice until the water runs perfectly clear. While this practice is becoming less crucial, traditionally rice would be coated with talc for shipping so it would not absorb moisture and stick together; it obviously was necessary to make sure the water was clear and the rice was pure before beginning the cooking process. To wash the rice, you can either place it in a sieve and rinse it under cold running water, stirring it around as you rinse, or place it in the pot in which it will be cooked and continue to rinse and drain it until the water is clear. If your sink is white it will be difficult to see the white starch, so I would suggest using the pot method. If your sink is stainless steel, then either method will work well.

COOKING THE RICE

Once the rice is ready for cooking, there are three ways in which it can be cooked. How much water to add to the rice is always open to debate. The method I use is one suggested by famed fusion chef Ming Tsai, whose Blue Ginger restaurant in suburban Boston is a mecca for foodies. He terms it the Mount Fuji Method. Place the rice in whatever cooker you are using and place your hand on top of it flat. Then fill the pot with water until the water reaches the knuckle nearest your palm on your index finger. Somewhat less romantic but always accurate is to add 1 cup of water for each 1 cup of raw rice.

Some authorities advocate soaking the rice in the cold water for 30 minutes after rinsing to soften the grains before cooking it. If time permits, I add this step to the process, but I ignore it if time is short.

By far, the best way to cook rice is in an electric rice cooker; the fact that this appliance is a fixture in almost every Asian household around the world should be enough of an endorsement. The rice cooker does not have to cost more than $25 or $30, and there are many options on the market. The rice cooker also doubles as a vegetable steamer, and most come with a basket to accomplish that task.

All you have to do is plug in the rice cooker, turn it on, and the cooker takes it from that point forward. It will cook the rice and then turn itself off or down to a warm setting.

An alternative that also works well is a slow cooker. Unlike the rice cooker, the slow cooker does not know when to turn itself off—you have to help it. But like the rice cooker, the chances of burning the rice are negligible because the heat is so low.

If you're using a slow cooker, set it on High, and use these times as a guide:

1 cup of rice for 1½ hours
2 cups of rice for 2 hours
3 cups of rice for 2¼ hours

The last, and least desirable, method is to cook the rice on top of the stove. Make sure the pot you are using is heavy and that the lid fits tightly. Bring the pot to a boil over medium heat, and after the rice starts to boil, turn the heat down to low. Do not remove the lid, and *never* stir sushi rice as it cooks because stirring will cause it to release starch. After 15 to 20 minutes, reduce the heat to its lowest possible setting for 5 minutes, then turn off the heat.

With all of these methods, allow the rice to sit undisturbed for 15 minutes before continuing. If you're using an electric rice cooker, learn how long your particular cooker takes to cook so you will know when it has turned itself down to the warm setting.

SEASONING THE RICE

While the rice is cooking, prepare your seasoning mixture. Here is your basic formula:

COOKED RICE	RICE VINEGAR	SUGAR	KOSHER SALT
5 to 7 cups	¼ cup	1 tablespoon	1½ teaspoons
7 to 9 cups	6 tablespoons	4½ teaspoons	2 teaspoons
9 to 11 cups	½ cup	2 tablespoons	2½ teaspoons

Stir this mixture together until it becomes clear, which signals that the sugar and salt have dissolved. If you prefer, you can make a large amount of dressing in advance and refrigerate it for up to a week. Allow the portion you are using to reach room temperature before using; you do not want to pour chilled dressing over the hot rice.

Turn the rice into the container you are using to season it by running the paddle around the rim of the pan to loosen the cooked rice, and then invert it. Sprinkle the vinegar mixture all over the rice by pouring it onto the back of the paddle. Then wait about 10 seconds to allow the liquid to be absorbed by the hot rice.

Use the paddle in an up-and-down cutting motion to spread the rice into a thin, even layer; do not stir the rice to avoid breaking the grains. After the rice is spread into an even layer, gently turn over small portions to allow steam to escape.

COOLING THE RICE

The final step in preparing the rice is to fan it to speed the cooling process, which creates the proper texture. Continue to turn over small portions of rice, and then cool the mixture with your other hand with a fan or even a magazine. An alternative is to use a small electric fan. After about 4 to 5 minutes there should be no steam visible, at which point the rice is cool enough to cover.

To keep the rice ready to use for up to 6 hours, wring out a clean lint-free tea towel, and completely cover the rice tub or mixing bowl. At this point the sushi rice is ready to roll or form; check the towel every hour or so to make sure that it has not dried out.

Slicing Fish

THE IMPORTANCE OF USING ONLY THE FINEST sushi-quality fish is discussed on page 13; now that you have the fish at home it is time to slice it. But how you slice it depends on what form of sushi you are making. Before cutting the fish, go over it carefully with your fingers, and remove any remaining pin bones with tweezers or a vegetable peeler.

To cut fish successfully, your knife must be incredibly sharp, or it will squish the fish down and the slices will not be attractive. I find that it is easier to cut fish that is partially frozen; place the fish on a sheet of plastic wrap and place it in the freezer for 30 to 45 minutes, depending on thickness. Alternatively, if you have taken frozen fish out to thaw, probe it until you believe you can get a knife through it, and slice it then.

The general rule is to slice across the grain of the fish; this ensures that the resulting slice is tender and has a cross-cut grain pattern. Lay your knife on the fish at the very back end part of the blade. Draw the blade across the fish in one long stroke to complete the slice. If you do not complete the slice in one stroke, lift the knife out of the cut and carefully repeat the slicing motion in the same direction. Avoid using a sawing motion, as this could damage the fish.

For *nigiri-zushi*, the goal is to create a pliable slice of fish that will drape nicely over the rice. To do that, cut the fish into diagonal slices about ¼ inch thick. Hold your knife at a 45-degree angle to the fish, and rest the fingers of your other hand lightly on the fish. Start at the side of the fillet rather than from the head or tail portion.

For all types of *maki*, the goal is to create thin logs. Cut the fish as described above, but make the slices ⅓ inch thick. Then cut each slice of fish lengthwise into ⅓-inch strips. For *temaki-zushi*, the strips should be about 3 inches long, but for *maki* they can be left the length of the initial strip; save any trimmings to fill in the *maki* later.

The goal when cutting fish for *oshi-zushi* is to create large, flat slices that can be placed on the bottom of the mold. Hold your knife parallel to the fillet, and slice it as thin as you can; slices about ⅛ inch thick are the goal.

When arranging pieces of fish for a serving of *chirashi-zushi,* the fish should be cut straight down in ½-inch strips rather than at an angle, and from there it can be cut into small squares to arrange.

Preparing Shrimp

WHILE SHRIMP CURLING AROUND THE EDGES OF A FLUTED CUP for a shrimp cocktail is attractive, that is not what you want when using shrimp in sushi; you want them to be straight and flat as a topping or filling. The way to achieve this is almost diametrically opposed to how you prepare shrimp for other cuisines. The shrimp are deveined from the underside, which almost cuts the shrimp in half, rather than removing the vein from the top.

The best size shrimp to use for *nigiri-zushi* is large, which are sold as 21 to 25 per pound; shrimp that are larger will be too much to eat in one bite. For *futomaki* and other thick rolls, use large prawns. With all the methods, remain constant.

Hold each shrimp with the legs up, and insert a bamboo skewer underneath the transparent shell between the two pairs of legs; be careful not to pierce the flesh if at all possible. Then cook the shrimp by bringing a large pot of salted water to a boil over high heat.

Add the shrimp, cover the pan, and when the water returns to a boil, remove the pan from the heat. Allow the shrimp to sit undisturbed for 5 minutes, and then drain the shrimp. When cool enough to handle, remove the skewers and peel the shrimp.

Place the shrimp on a cutting board with the vein side down, and cut along the underside of the shrimp with a sharp knife until you reach the dark vein; you will almost cut the shrimp in half. Scrape out the vein with a wooden skewer, and then trim off the ends of the shrimp to give them a neater appearance.

Preparing Vegetables

THE CONTRAST OF SOFT, BUTTERY FISH WITH CRUNCHY RAW or blanched vegetables adds textural interest to eating sushi, and most thick *maki* rolls include at least one vegetable. As was true with fish and seafood, the form of sushi in which the vegetable will be used determines how it should be cut. For any roll the goal is to form a thin log or triangle, while for vegetables to top fingers of *nigiri* the vegetables should be oval, and for pressed pieces of *oshi-zushi* they should be thin slices cut to fit the mold.

If rolling a *maki,* you are in luck if you are using pencil-thin stalks of asparagus or individual green beans; these vegetables should be blanched in boiling water for just 30 to 40 seconds, depending on thickness, then plunged into a bowl of ice water to stop the cooking process and to set the bright green color.

Whether or not to blanch vegetables such as carrots or strips of bell pepper is a matter of personal choice. If you choose to do so, blanch these sturdier vegetables for 1 to 2 minutes.

Cucumber is the most popular vegetable included in sushi, and preparing it is a variation on the old adage of pushing a round plug into a square hole; in this case you are trimming the round plug so that it becomes square. Begin by cutting a section as long as your sheet of *nori*. Then, using a long vegetable knife, cut off all four sides so that the cucumber sits firmly on the counter. Cut it into ¼-inch slices. Turn the slices over, and cut again until you have ¼-inch strips.

If you want to create slivers, called julienne in Western cooking, the basic procedure remains the same, but the initial slices should be as thin as possible. After the slices are made, cut them into very thin strips in the other direction. For diced vegetables, make slivers and then cut the resulting strips into ¼-inch slices.

For vegetables that are shredded, such as carrot and *daikon,* feel free to use the holes of a box grater to do the job. Or if you own a Japanese mandoline, you can achieve professional looking shreds effortlessly. If you do not want to take the time to shred vegetables to top a bowl of scattered sushi, you can substitute thin sprouts such as radish or alfalfa.

Making *a Tamago*

MANY SUSHI AFICIONADOS BELIEVE that being able to create an excellent *tamago*, the sweet egg omelet that is essential to sushi, is the mark of a good chef, and there is no reason why you should not list yourself among the finest. If you can scramble an egg, you can make an excellent *tamago*. While the traditional square pan, *makiyakinabe*, automatically creates the right shape, you can use a round pan and then trim the resulting omelet into a square shape.

TRADITIONAL *TAMAGO*

PREP: **5** MINUTES
COOK: **10** MINUTES

MAKES **1** OMELET

4 large eggs, well beaten
¼ cup *dashi* stock (page 23) or water
1 tablespoon granulated sugar
1 tablespoon *mirin*
½ teaspoon kosher salt
1 tablespoon vegetable oil

1. Combine eggs, *dashi*, sugar, *mirin*, and salt in a large bowl; whisk well.
2. Heat oil in a 12-inch skillet over medium heat, tilting the pan to cover all areas. Remove excess with paper towel, and set paper towel aside.
3. Add one-third of egg mixture to skillet so that it creates a thin layer. Reduce heat to medium-low, and cook until the surface begins to set and the edges begin to crisp.
4. Using chopsticks or a fork, fold omelet beginning at the back toward you in 2-inch sections. Push folded omelet to far end of pan.

5. Wipe inside of pan with reserved paper towel. Add one-third of remaining egg mixture to pan, and tilt to cover the bottom. Gently lift cooked omelet to allow mixture underneath to cook. When egg begins to set, roll as before.

6. Repeat process one more time, at which point all egg should be cooked. Remove pan from heat, and allow omelet to cool before removing it from pan.

Note: Omelet can be prepared up to 1 day in advance and refrigerated, tightly covered with plastic wrap.

Making Tempura

CRUNCHY FRIED FOODS ADD ANOTHER TEXTURAL ELEMENT to *maki* rolls, and can also be included as part of the topping for scattered sushi. The most common foods fried are shrimp and soft-shell crabs, but any thin vegetable is another option. While there is a traditional *tempura* pan available, you can fry foods for sushi in any pan you would use for french fries or fritters.

TEMPURA

PREP: 5 MINUTES PLUS 30 MINUTES CHILLING
FRY: 4 MINUTES

MAKES 2 CUPS BATTER

1 large egg
1 cup ice-cold seltzer or sparkling water
$\frac{1}{2}$ cup rice flour
$\frac{1}{2}$ cup cake flour
$\frac{1}{2}$ teaspoon salt
$\frac{1}{2}$ cup all-purpose flour
4 to 6 cups vegetable oil

1. In a large bowl, beat egg with seltzer until thoroughly combined. Quickly whisk in rice flour, cake flour, and salt. Refrigerate batter for 30 minutes.

2. Place all-purpose flour in a medium bowl. Pour oil into saucepan or wok, and heat over medium-high heat to a temperature of 375°F; at the proper temperature a bread cube placed in oil will bubble furiously and brown in 10 to 12 seconds.

3. Working in batches, quickly dip food to be fried in flour, shaking off any excess; then roll food in tempura batter, allowing excess to drain off. Transfer food to oil using tongs. Cook until crisp and light golden brown, $1\frac{1}{2}$ to 2 minutes. Using a slotted spoon, transfer to a paper towel–lined plate to drain. Set aside and use as directed in individual sushi recipes.

Making *Dashi*

DASHI IS THE CHICKEN STOCK OF JAPANESE COOKING; it is used not only as the basis for almost all soups but also as a key ingredient in hundreds of recipes, including the *tamago* omelet used in many forms of sushi. There actually are two versions, and both are flavored with dried bonito tuna flakes (*katsuo-boshi*) and a piece of *kombu*, a type of kelp seaweed. The goal in making *dashi* is to achieve a perfectly clear broth. *Dashi* Number One is stronger, and is the base for all clear soups (*suimono*). *Dashi* Number Two is more diluted because it is made from the ingredients already steeped for Number One; it is the base for popular soups made with *miso* paste, a soybean derivative.

While some of the subtle flavor will diminish, *dashi* can be refrigerated for up to 4 days or frozen for up to 3 months. It is a good idea to freeze it in portion sizes you use frequently, and for small amounts freeze some in ice cube trays.

DASHI NUMBER ONE

PREP: **5** MINUTES PLUS **2** HOURS SOAKING
COOK: **5** MINUTES

MAKES: **1** QUART

1 (4-inch) square *kombu*
4 cups cold water
¾ cup bonito flakes (*katsuo-boshi*)

1. Wipe white film off *kombu,* and soak in 3½ cups water for 2 hours. Bring water to a boil over medium-high heat. When it comes to a boil, remove pan from heat, and remove *kombu;* set aside and reserve for *Dashi* Number Two.

2. Add remaining ½ cup cold water to pan, and then sprinkle bonito flakes on top. Use a spoon or chopsticks to force them to bottom of pan, and allow mixture to steep for 3 minutes.

3. Line a strainer with a double layer of cheesecloth or a paper coffee filter, and slowly pour stock through it, pressing down gently. Reserve bonito flakes for making *Dashi* Number Two.

Note: For a stronger stock, simmer *dashi* for up to 5 minutes.

DASHI NUMBER TWO

PREP: **5** MINUTES
COOK: **15** MINUTES

MAKES: **1** QUART

4 cups water
Reserved *kombu* and bonito flakes from making *Dashi* Number One

1. In a 2-quart saucepan, combine water, *kombu,* and bonito flakes. Bring to a boil over medium-high heat, stirring occasionally.
2. Reduce heat to low and simmer for 15 minutes.
3. Line a strainer with a double layer of cheesecloth or a paper coffee filter, and slowly pour stock through it, pressing down gently. Discard solids.

SEASONING DEEP-FRIED TOFU (*ABURA-AGE*)

While pieces of deep-fried tofu can be split apart like pita bread and then stuffed with seasoned rice and myriad ingredients, it does taste better if it is seasoned first; the step takes but minutes.

Cut each piece in half diagonally to turn it into 2 triangles. Place the triangles in a strainer and pour boiling water over both sides to get rid of excess oil. Then heat ½ cup *Dashi* Number One (page 23), ¼ cup soy sauce, ¼ cup *mirin,* and 1 tablespoon granulated sugar in a saucepan; heat over medium-high heat until it comes to a boil.

Simmer triangles, uncovered, for 15 minutes. Then drain, and allow to reach room temperature before filling. You can save the poaching liquid and refrigerate it, tightly covered, for up to 1 week.

MAKING *WASABI* PASTE

Although tubes of prepared *wasabi* are sold in many supermarkets, I believe the flavor from a high-quality powder is far better. Mix equal parts of powder and water together in a small bowl, and let it sit for at least 10 minutes to allow the flavor to develop. If making more than a few tablespoons, add the water gradually. Keep the paste covered with plastic wrap to keep the aroma, or you can do it the Japanese way and turn the bowl upside down; if the paste has the right consistency it will not drip.

Toasting Sesame Seeds

WHILE BLACK SESAME SEEDS CAN BE USED right out of the package as a garnish, white sesame seeds disappear into the white rice unless they are toasted. Toasting also releases the oils and adds to their aroma and flavor. There are two ways to toast them:

➤ Preheat the oven to 350°F, and place sesame seeds on a baking sheet. Bake for 5 to 7 minutes, or until lightly browned.

➤Place sesame seeds in a small dry skillet and cook over medium heat, stirring frequently, for 2 to 3 minutes, or until lightly browned.

Garnishes

THERE ARE ENTIRE BOOKS WRITTEN ON THE SUBJECT of Japanese garnishing, and I would not presume to give you a comprehensive course. But there are some garnishes that are very easy to make, and they dress up sushi plates enormously. Garnishes fall into two basic categories—there are those that are intended to be eaten as part of the meal and others that are only intended as decoration. Here are a few that will wow guests:

Making a *wasabi* leaf: For each leaf, create 1 tablespoon of *wasabi* by mixing 1 tablespoon powder with 1 tablespoon water, and allow the mixture to set up for 10 minutes. Form the paste into a cylinder 1½ inches long by rolling the paste between the palms of your hands. Place the cylinder on a plate, and flatten it with your fingers. Pinch one end to create a stem, and then mold the remaining paste into a leaf form. Cut in a central vein and side veins at a 45-degree angle using the tip of a knife or a toothpick.

Making a pickled ginger rose: Lay slices of pickled ginger horizontally on a plate with the edges slightly overlapping. Roll the slices into a cylinder, and then turn it over onto a plate, pressing the layers out to resemble a flower.

Making a cucumber branch: Cut a 2½-inch section of Japanese cucumber, and then cut the section in half lengthwise so it sits securely on the counter. Cut the peel off of the sides, and then slice the cucumber into ⅛ inch lengthwise slices, stopping ½ inch from the bottom to create a base. Carefully fold back each of the cut strips into the gap between itself and the next strip; leave the last strip free.

Making a radish cup: Cut the base off of a large red radish, and make 3 cuts down the radish at a 45-degree angle. Remove the core of the radish, and soak the cup in ice water for 15 minutes to allow the petals to expand.

Making flower petals: This garnish of thinly sliced hard vegetables like carrots, cucumber, or *daikon* is easy *if* you purchase flower-shaped cutters; they are available in both Western gourmet shops and Asian markets. Cut a chunk of vegetable to a length of 1½ inches, making sure the bottom is flat to sit securely on a counter; press the cutter through the vegetable. Then remove the cutter and slice the vegetable into very thin slices using a very sharp paring knife.

Making a tomato flower: This garnish is also lovely for any Western-style dish. Peel a tomato with a very sharp paring knife beginning at the stem end, cutting the peel into a continuous ½-inch strip and stopping before you reach the other end; you want a flat base for the flower. Place the base on a plate, and then begin spiraling the peel into a circle from the outside in. You can use this flower as a holder for a cone of *wasabi* or place a pile of pickled ginger inside of it.

three ALL FORMS SUSHI

I f you read Chapter 2 carefully, then you now know everything essential to becoming a sushi superstar. This chapter demystifies sushi making; it is really not difficult at all once the rice is cooked and seasoned.

The secret to making professional-looking sushi is to prep all your ingredients to the proper size, and not be too generous with either the rice or ingredient additions. If you keep in mind that each piece of sushi or slice of *maki* is intended to be eaten in one bite, then you are not as likely to make them too large.

The various sections of this chapter will give you the skills to make each distinct form of sushi, and feel free to experiment with toppings and fillings. While you will find specific recipes in Chapter 4 for all of these forms, at the conclusion of each section in this chapter I offer suggestions for appropriate foods.

If you are nervous about your first ventures into sushi making, thinking about complex rolls or sculpted fingers, begin with platters or individual plates of scattered sushi (*chirashi-zushi*). Once you feel comfortable with the technique of making the rice, you will have more confidence to move on down the list of forms.

Preliminary Setup

BEGIN BY GETTING YOURSELF ORGANIZED WITH A BOWL of sushi rice covered with a damp towel, a bowl of tepid water into which you have poured rice vinegar at a ratio of 5 parts water to 1 part vinegar so you can clean your hands between pieces, and another damp towel on which you will dab your fingers after the dip into the bowl. If you dip your hands between pieces of sushi, the rice will not stick to them.

Next assemble all your other ingredients, including a small dish of *wasabi*, and you will be working like a well-oiled sushi machine in a matter of minutes. It actually takes far longer to slice and dice the toppings and fillings than it does to make the sushi.

If the sushi does not contain raw fish or other very perishable items, it can sit loosely covered with plastic wrap for up to a few hours before serving. But never refrigerate sushi; it will ruin the texture and flavor of the rice.

And there's nothing like practice to increase your speed. The first time I made a "battleship" it was hardly one I wanted to share with guests. But after about a dozen they started looking great. So for your first forays into sushi making, it is a good idea to have only close friends around.

The Finger Family

THESE THREE FORMS OF SUSHI ARE ALL FORMED into ovals or balls and then topped with an ingredient. While traditionally they are made by hand, a mold can be used for a few of them as well.

NIGIRI-ZUSHI (FINGER SUSHI)

Tamago *Nigiri-zushi*

Shrimp *Nigiri-zushi*

Barbecued Eel *Nigiri-zushi*

Salmon *Nigiri-zushi*

It is this form of sushi, developed in the nineteenth century, which created the modern genre as we know it today, so we will begin here. In Japanese, *nigiri* literally means "to gently squeeze," and that is what you'll be doing to form these fingers of seasoned rice, which serve as edible pedestals for a wide range of toppings called *neta*. It is important that the topping is supple so that it drapes well on top of the rice; a slice of raw carrot would not be a good candidate, while the same thin slice of carrot blanched works extremely well.

You will form *nigiri* from the top down, and then turn it over. Pick up a piece of topping, and rub one side with a dab of *wasabi* if desired. This dab traditionally is used for all forms of raw and cooked fish and seafood, but it certainly is optional if you are going to top the finger with a slice of *tamago* omelet.

Then pick up 1½ to 2 tablespoons of seasoned rice, and press it gently into the back of the topping, forming it into an oval. Be careful to not break the rice; if your sushi rice has the proper consistency, it should stay together without firm pressure. The last step is to press gently on the bottom of the finger so it will appear to have a slight hump when you set the topping up on the plate. Then turn the piece upside down with the topping now on top, and place it on a plate.

Molding the Fingers

While sushi chefs would never consider using the convenience of a mold to create fingers, it really makes perfect *nigiri* foolproof if you do so, and you can make a number at a time. The molds are made from plastic, and most create 5 pieces at a time. When using a mold, however, the method will be the reverse because you will create the fingers and then drape the topping over them.

Cut a sheet of plastic wrap about twice the size of your mold, drape it over the mold, and press the plastic wrap into the indentations. Then take rice and press it into the indentations gently up to the top of the mold, rewetting your fingers between indentations as necessary. Fold the plastic wrap over the top of the mold, and press on the cover.

Remove the lid, and fold back the plastic wrap. Then turn the mold over onto a plate, remove the mold, and pull up on the sides of the plastic wrap. Continue in this fashion until you have formed the number you want, keeping the completed sushi loosely covered with plastic wrap and not touching each other to prevent them from sticking together. You can allow them to sit at room temperature for a few hours, but do not refrigerate them.

Just prior to serving, rub your topping with *wasabi*, if desired, and drape the toppings over the fingers, pressing them on gently.

Good Choices to Top *Nigiri-zushi*: Slices of any raw fish (see page 19 for directions on how to cut the fish), shrimp cooked according to the method on page 20, roasted red bell pepper, grilled shiitake mushrooms, slices of *tamago* omelet tied with a ¼ inch strip of *nori*, or barbecued eel tied with a ¼ inch strip of *nori*.

Red Snapper *Nigiri-zushi*   **Yellowtail** *Nigiri-zushi*

GUNKAN-ZUSHI ("BATTLESHIP" SUSHI)

Gunkan-Zushi **topped with Tobiko**   *Gunkan-Zushi* **topped with Salmon Roe**

These "battleships" are a variation on fingers that is used when the toppings are tiny and could fall off the rice, or the toppings do not have enough structure to hold together. The fingers are wrapped in a sheet of *nori,* which creates a ¼ inch collar to encase the toppings.

Cut as many sheets of *nori* as necessary into strips 1 inch wide by 7 inches long, and set them aside in a dry place. Then make the fingers using one of the two methods detailed for *Nigiri-zushi,* but do not "hump" the rice; keep it even.

If your hands are wet, dry them well. Place a finger of rice on a plate, and wrap a strip of *nori* around it with the shiny side of the *nori* showing. The *nori* should be even with the bottom of the finger and extend about ¼ inch over the top. If the nori is too long and overlaps by more than ⅓ inch, you can either flatten the rice slightly to increase its circumference or trim the *nori.*

Then pick up a few grains of rice with a teaspoon, and place them at the end of the strip on the inside; they will act as glue for the *nori.* Press the strip into the rice, and continue until all your rice fingers are wrapped. Rub some *wasabi* on top of the rice, and then add the topping to the upper edge of the *nori.*

The last step is to garnish one end of the oval with an herb or vegetable that sticks up about ½ inch over the topping. I like to use small fans of cucumber, but you can also use sections of scallion greens, chives, or any other herb sprig.

While the fingers can be made a few hours in advance, the *nori* will only remain crisp for a brief time, so wrap and fill the sushi just prior to serving.

Good Choices to Top *Gunkan-zushi*: Any fish roe (traditional choices are large red eggs of salmon roe, tiny eggs of flying fish roe—called *tobiko*—or golden whitefish caviar), raw oysters or clams that can be rested on a dollop of cocktail sauce in lieu of *wasabi*, or nontraditional toppings such as Mexican guacamole or salsa.

TEMARI-ZUSHI (ROUND BALL SUSHI)

These perfectly round balls are formed in a sheet of plastic wrap, and they are a modern adaptation of *nigiri-zushi*. Begin by cutting an 8 inch square of plastic wrap, and place whatever ingredients you want to have showing in the center of the square; rub these ingredients with *wasabi* before placing them on the plastic. Then form a ball from 1½ to 2 tablespoons of sushi rice, and place the ball over the toppings, centering the ball on the toppings.

Pull up the plastic wrap around the toppings, twisting it to shape the rice and toppings into a ball. Unwrap the ball, and turn it over so that the toppings are showing, and then repeat as many times as you would like, changing the sheet of plastic wrap if the rice begins to stick or the toppings leave a residue.

Good Choices to Top *Temari-zushi*: Any raw fish or crispy vegetable cut into ¼ inch dice.

Rolling *Maki-zushi*

MAKING INDIVIDUAL PIECES OF SUSHI such as those described in the above sections is far more labor intensive than making and slicing up *maki* rolls; in just about the same amount of time you have eight individual pieces instead of one. These rolls are the assembly line of sushi making.

There is a great range of options for *maki-zushi;* the rolls can be thin or thick, and the rice can be on the inside or on the outside. The only constant is that each roll contains a half or whole sheet of *nori* and they are rolled into either a round shape or formed into a square. Most of the thin rolls contain only one ingredient; the thicker versions are visually stunning, and they can contain up to 4 or 5 ingredients of various colors and textures.

In this section you will learn how to make them all; the technique is the same. Your key piece of equipment is a bamboo sushi mat, called a *makisu*, like the one described on page 12. You will also need plastic wrap, and you need to begin the process with your rice already seasoned and your other ingredients ready to roll.

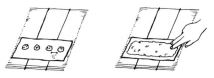

A technique common to all types of rolls is what I call the patchwork approach to layering the rice on the *nori*. Keeping your hands moist—but not dripping wet—dot the surface of the section of *nori* to be covered with a few teaspoons of rice placed at ½ inch intervals. Then pat the rice down so that it forms an even layer. By using this method there is very little chance of ripping the *nori*, and it is possible to keep the rice layer thin.

HOSOMAKI-ZUSHI (THIN ROLLS)

Cucumber *Hosomaki-zushi* and Tuna *Hosomaki-zushi*

These thin rolls are less than 1 inch in diameter, which makes them great hors d'oeuvres for a cocktail party. You'll use only a half sheet of *nori* and ½ cup of sushi rice for each roll.

Place the bamboo mat on the counter in front of you with the slats going horizontally; you will be rolling the roll away from you. Then place the *nori* with its shiny side down on the mat, leaving 3 slats uncovered to use as your guiding edge.

Spread the rice as detailed above, leaving a ½ inch border on the far side. If using *wasabi*, spread a thin line down the middle of the rice, and then arrange your filling in the center of the rice; it should go the length of the *nori*, so paste together a few pieces if necessary. If you're using more than one strip, push them as close together as possible, and angle-cut the ends so that they join smoothly.

Lift the mat with your thumbs while pressing the filling into the rice with the rest of your fingers. Roll the mat over the filling, stopping when the mat reaches the far side of the roll. Work as quickly as possible so that the filling does not slide out, and keep pressure on the roll even between your two hands.

The next part of the procedure is what tightens the roll. Pull the partially completed roll toward you with one hand while the other hand holds the mat taut. Then open the mat, and move the roll back to the edge in front of you, leaving 3 slats uncovered by the roll.

Finish the roll by rolling it again until the free edge of the *nori* is covered and adheres. Take the roll out of the mat, and place it seam side down on a plate; if the *nori* had not completely adhered, it will after sitting for a few minutes from the moisture in the rice. If you are not thrilled with the shape of the roll, now is the time to act. Use the bamboo mat and adjust the shape from the top to make it rounder or more square, depending on your preference.

Cut the roll into 8 pieces with a very sharp knife; cut it first in half, and then cut each half into 4 equal slices. Wipe your knife with a damp cloth between slices to keep the knife from getting sticky and crushing the roll.

Good Choices to Roll in *Hosomaki-zushi*: Strips of any raw fish cut into ⅓ inch logs; tuna is a common choice, called *tekka-maki* and named for a hot iron that is the same color as red tuna. Many types of vegetables are also used, the most common one being cucumber; they are called *kappa-maki,* named for a Japanese water imp, and are used to cleanse the palate between pieces of fish. Other good choices are logs of *tamago,* or even nontraditional choices like strips of cooked chicken.

FUTOMAKI-ZUSHI (THICK ROLLS)

Tamago, **Steamed Carrot, and Asparagus** *Futomaki*

The procedure is the same for rolling thick rolls as for rolling thin ones. The differences are that you use a whole sheet of *nori,* more rice, and more ingredients. Use 1 cup of sushi rice for a thick roll, and leave a 2-inch border of the *nori* without filling.

When assembling the ingredients to place in the center of the roll, place them in the center of the rice rather than in the center of the sheet of *nori.* This will keep them centered once the *maki* is rolled.

Good Choices to Roll in *Futomaki-zushi*: There are many recipes in Chapter 4 that give you specific combinations and ways to prepare them. If you want to experiment, choose ingredients with contrasting colors and textures. If using a fish, choose it first, and then build the remaining ingredients around that choice. For example, a combination of *hamachi* with steamed asparagus and creamy avocado would make a pleasing contrast.

URAMAKI-ZUSHI (INSIDE-OUT ROLLS)

Barbecued Eel with Carrot and *Tamago Uramaki-zushi*

It is always very showy to serve inside-out rolls, which means the rice is on the outside rather than the inside. Once rolled, you can coat the rolls with toasted sesame seeds, *tobiko* or other small fish roe, or a finely chopped herb such as cilantro or chives. The good news is that they are no more difficult to make than any other roll, perhaps even easier because the rice holds them together naturally.

Cover your bamboo mat with plastic wrap to keep the sticky rice from adhering to the mat and not itself. Place the bamboo mat on the counter in front of you with the slats going horizontally; you will be rolling the roll away from you.

Place a full sheet of *nori* with its shiny side down on the mat, leaving 3 slats uncovered to use as your guiding edge. Spread about 1 cup of sushi rice on top, using the patchwork method described on page 34. If the rice starts to cling to your fingertips, dip your hands into the bowl of vinegared water again.

Then rinse your fingers again and turn over the sheet so that the rice is face down on the plastic-covered mat. Rub a line of *wasabi* down the center of the *nori*, and place your chosen fillings on top of the *nori*, about one third of the way up from the bottom edge.

Lift the mat with your thumbs while holding the filling with the rest of your fingers. Roll the mat over the filling, stopping when the mat reaches the far side of the roll. Work as quickly as possible so that the filling does not slide out, and keep pressure on the roll even between your two hands.

The next part of the procedure is what tightens the roll. Pull the partially completed roll toward you with one hand while the other hand holds the mat taut. Then open the mat, and move the roll back to the edge in front of you, leaving 3 slats uncovered by the roll. Now finish by rolling it again until the free edge of rice-coated *nori* is covered and adheres.

Take the roll out of the mat, and place it on a plate; make sure the rolls do not touch, or they may stick together. If you are not thrilled with the shape of the roll, now is the time to act. Use the bamboo mat to adjust the shape from the top to make it rounder or more square, depending on your preference. At this point you can garnish the roll if you choose to do so.

Wrap the roll in plastic wrap, which facilitates slicing, and cut the roll into 8 pieces with a very sharp knife; cut it first in half, and then cut each half into 4 equal slices. Wipe your knife with a damp cloth between slices to keep the knife from getting sticky and crushing the roll. Remove the plastic wrap from each piece, and serve.

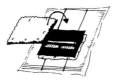 

Good Choices to Roll in *Uramaki-zushi*: As with the thick rolls above, there are many recipes in Chapter 4 that give you specific combinations and ways to prepare them, including the nontraditional but very popular California roll.

TEMAKI-ZUSHI (HAND ROLLS)

Hand rolls are do-it-yourself sushi. Half-sheets of *nori* are filled with sushi rice and whatever other foods you choose, and then rolled into a cone; think of them as Japanese tacos or savory ice cream cones. Hand rolls are a great way to entertain friends at a buffet dinner; all you have to do is put out sheets of *nori*, a bowl of sushi rice, and a selection of other ingredients, and let the guests compile creations according to personal preference.

One caution is that hand rolls should be eaten right after they are made; the *nori* changes from crisp to soggy within a few minutes and can become cumbersome to eat.

Here is how to make them: Cut the sheets of *nori* in half to form rectangles 4 by 7 inches. Lay 1 piece across the counter or on a plate horizontally, and pat ½ cup of sushi rice on the diagonal across one of the shorter sides. Then add the fillings to the center of the rice, pressing the ingredients into the rice.

Now comes the rolling step: Fold the uncovered corner beneath the rice over the fillings, and roll the *nori* into a cone. Voilà! You now have a hand roll.

Good Choices to Roll in *Temaki-zushi:* The main difference between fillings for hand rolls and thick or inside-out rolls is that the ingredients should be sliced into pieces that are about 4 inches long rather than the 7 inches for other rolls. But like other rolls, use a combination of foods, and do consult the recipes in Chapter 4.

Bountiful Bowls (*Chirashi-zushi*)

IF YOU ENJOY THE LUSCIOUS TASTE AND TEXTURE of sushi rice and the wide variety of ingredients that can be enjoyed with it, and want a meal in a bowl quickly without fuss, then *chirashi-zushi*—literally "scattered sushi"—is tailor-made for your needs. These bowls are also a good way to start making sushi because they require no skills other than making the rice properly. There are two primary types—*edomae chirashi-zushi* hails from Tokyo and the Kansai style is called *gomoku-zushi.*

Either type of scattered sushi can be served in individual portions or in a large bowl for a group, allowing diners to choose what they would like to sample. It should go without saying that scattered sushi must be eaten with chopsticks (or a fork); this is clearly not finger food. For tips on chopstick etiquette, see page 70.

EDOMAE CHIRASHI-ZUSHI

Even though there is no technique mastery involved in creating scattered sushi, there is a strong aesthetic component. In this style, all the ingredients are placed on top of the rice so they need to be arranged like a still-life painting with contrasting color and shapes. But the assembly is not random; all pieces of the same food should be grouped together.

The sushi rice is placed in the bowl, to a level of about two-thirds full. Then the ancillary ingredients are artfully arranged on top. Think of the top of the rice as a horizontal canvas, and begin juxtaposing colors and textures on top of it. Slices of raw fish can be decoratively folded or turned into small flowers, and vegetables should be cut in decorative patterns.

GOMOKU-ZUSHI

The Kansai version of scattered sushi is more free-form, and most of the ingredients are gently mixed into the rice, with some pieces reserved for a garnish. This form is usually served on a plate rather than in a bowl, and the pieces of food are cut into small sizes to make it easier to eat with chopsticks. The garnish pieces can be left larger, but not too large to eat comfortably in one or two bites.

Good Choices for *Chirashi-zushi*: An advantage to making one large bowl is that up to five different species of fish can be used, but you should also always include some vegetables to balance the fish in color and texture. Consult the recipes in Chapter 4 for specific suggestions. The *gomoku-zushi* is the pot pie of the sushi world; you can use any bits of leftover this and that.

Pressed Sushi (*Oshi-zushi*)

THE JAPANESE ARE PURISTS ABOUT AESTHETICS, but they, too, like some shortcuts. Those perfect rectangular logs of *oshi-zushi* (pressed sushi) that you see on menus are made in a mold. Traditionally these molds were made from wood, but there are now many inexpensive plastic versions on the market.

A traditional mold comes in three parts; there is a base, a rectangular box that fits over the base, and a lid with which to press the sushi. On most molds the rectangular box is marked with grooves to facilitate cutting the sushi into pieces before removing it from the mold.

It is also easy to improvise a mold using common kitchen equipment such as an individual loaf pan. Cut a sheet of heavy cardboard so that it fits inside the loaf pan, and wrap the cardboard in a few layers of plastic wrap. Line the loaf pan with plastic as well to facilitate removing the log of pressed sushi.

The ingredients for pressed sushi should be sliced paper-thin, but in wide enough strips to create a pattern on the top. For example, cucumbers should be sliced lengthwise or on a diagonal, and fish should be sliced thinly as for *sashimi*.

Rinse all pieces of the mold with water to make sure that the rice will not stick to it. Then place the base under the rectangle, press ½ cup sushi rice into the mold, and top it with a piece of *nori* cut to fit the mold; the *nori* provides stability to the resulting pieces. Press it down with the lid, and rinse the lid, if necessary, to get rid of any rice that stuck. Then arrange half of your filling ingredients on top of the *nori*, and press them down again with the lid. Repeat this process, arranging the ingredients on the top of the mold as artfully as possible, as that is the layer that people will see.

Press everything together firmly with the lid. Then remove the lid and slice part of the way down each mold, rinsing your knife with water between slices. Then replace the lid, and remove the sushi from the mold by pressing down on the lid as you lift the rectangle off. At this point you can complete the cutting process, and the sushi are ready to serve.

Oshi-zushi should only be served if diners are at a table. The pieces really are too large to maneuver as cocktail party finger food.

Good Choices for *Oshi-zushi*: Cooked seafood, such as lobster cut into thin medallions, as well as raw fish, are elegant when presented. Other options are thin slices of vegetables such as grilled eggplant or zucchini, as well as roasted red bell pepper. You'll also find specific recipes in Chapter 4.

Four SUSHI RECIPES *from* TRADITIONAL *to* CONTEMPORARY

A chapter of recipes for sushi is almost an oxymoron; most sushi is simply fish on top of rice or inside of rice. But there are times that you might want to vary the fare, or you may have questions as to the proportion of one ingredient to another—that is when you can consult the recipes in this chapter.

Feel free to experiment with forms. If you like a group of ingredients and prefer to join them in a thick *futomaki* rather than roll them into individual *temaki* hand rolls, go ahead and do it. Or rather than using a topping for a single piece of *nigiri-zushi*, you might want to create a thin *hosomaki* roll. Just keep the proportions of ingredients in mind.

Most of the traditional recipes will give you guidance for how to prepare ingredients, but once you start reading the recipes in the portion of this chapter titled Contemporary Concepts (page 56), you'll learn to throw authenticity to the wind! You will see how the various sushi forms described in Chapter 3 can be utilized with ingredients as non-Japanese as bacon and basil.

Preparation Time

EACH RECIPE LISTS PREPARATION TIME, along with any time needed to cook any ingredient. This preparation time assumes that there is a bowl of seasoned sushi rice already made and ready to go. Other component recipes found in Chapter 2, such as *Tempura* Batter or *Tamago*, however, are factored in to the prep time.

Vegetarian

RAW AND BLANCHED VEGETABLES MAKE FANTASTIC SUSHI; they are colorful and their crisp texture serves as a foil to the chewy rice. This group of recipes showcases the variety that can be included when making sushi.

GRILLED EGGPLANT *with* SESAME *NIGIRI-ZUSHI*

PREP: **10** MINUTES
GRILL: **4** MINUTES

MAKES **24** PIECES

1 tablespoon soy sauce
2 teaspoons toasted sesame oil
2 Japanese eggplants, sliced on the diagonal into ¼-inch slices
2½ cups seasoned sushi rice (page 18)
Wasabi to taste
3 tablespoons toasted sesame seeds (page 25)

1. Preheat a grill or oven broiler. In a small bowl, combine soy sauce and oil, and stir well. Brush mixture on both sides of eggplant slices, and grill for 2 minutes per side or until eggplant is softened.

2. To make sushi, follow the method on page 30, and then sprinkle completed pieces with sesame seeds.

CARROT *and* SCALLION *NIGIRI-ZUSHI*

PREP: **15** MINUTES
BOIL: **5** MINUTES

MAKES **24** PIECES

2 thick carrots, peeled and cut on the diagonal into ¼-inch slices
12 to 24 green scallion tops, depending on length
2½ cups seasoned sushi rice (page 18)
***Wasabi* to taste**

1. Bring a 2-quart saucepan of salted water to a boil over high heat. Add carrot slices and boil for 4 minutes, or until carrots are crisp-tender. Remove carrots from saucepan with a slotted spoon, and plunge them into ice water to stop the cooking action.

2. Add scallion tops to the saucepan and blanch for 15 seconds. Drain scallions, and add to ice water. Drain both carrots and scallions, and pat dry with paper towels.

3. To make sushi, follow the method on page 30. Place each piece on a scallion, and tie the scallion around the middle of the carrot with a knot on top.

RED BELL PEPPER *and* GREEN BEAN *HOSOMAKI*

PREP: **15** MINUTES
BOIL: **1½** MINUTES

MAKES **3** ROLLS (**24** PIECES)

½ red bell pepper, seeds and ribs removed, cut into ¼-inch slices
9 green beans, stemmed
1½ sheets *nori*
1½ cups seasoned sushi rice (page 18)
***Wasabi* to taste**

1. Bring a 2-quart saucepan of salted water to a boil over high heat. Add bell pepper strips and green beans, and boil for 1½ minutes. Drain vegetables and plunge them into ice water to stop the cooking action. Drain again, and pat dry with paper towels.

2. To make rolls, cut the full sheet of *nori* in half. Treat each sheet of *nori* with ½ cup seasoned rice, and spread *wasabi* on top of rice. Place red bell pepper slices and green beans on top of rice and roll according to the method on page 34.

Note: Pencil-thin asparagus can be substituted for green beans, and any color of bell pepper can be used, too.

TEMPURA VEGETABLE *FUTOMAKI*

PREP: **25** MINUTES PLUS **30** MINUTES CHILLING
FRY: **2** MINUTES

MAKES 3 ROLLS (24 PIECES)

VEGETABLES
Tempura Batter (page 22)
1 thin carrot
6 green beans
2 slices (¼-inch thick) sweet onion
3 cups vegetable oil
½ cup all-purpose flour

ROLL
3 sheets *nori*
3 cups seasoned sushi rice (page 18)
Wasabi to taste

1. Make *Tempura* Batter and chill it for 30 minutes.

2. Peel carrot and cut into ¼-inch batons 4 inches long. Stem green beans. Cut onion slices in half, and separate into slivers.

3. In a 10-inch skillet with high sides or a saucepan, heat oil to a temperature of 375°F over medium-high heat. Dip vegetables into flour, shaking off any excess, and then *tempura* batter; fry for 2 to 3 minutes, or until browned. Remove vegetables from oil with a slotted spoon, and drain on paper towels.

4. To make rolls, treat each sheet of *nori* with 1 cup seasoned rice, and spread *wasabi* on top of rice. Divide fried vegetables on top of rice, and roll according to the method on page 35.

WILD MUSHROOM *CHIRASHI-ZUSHI*

PREP: **15** MINUTES
SAUTÉ: **5** MINUTES

MAKES 4 SERVINGS

¼ pound fresh shiitake mushrooms
¼ pound fresh crimini mushrooms
¼ pound fresh enoki mushrooms
2 tablespoons toasted sesame oil
1 tablespoon soy sauce
3 cups seasoned sushi rice (page 18)
4 scallions, trimmed and thinly sliced
4 sprigs fresh watercress for garnish

1. Wipe shiitake, crimini, and enoki mushrooms with a damp paper towel. Discard stems from shiitake and crimini mushrooms, and slice thinly.
2. In a 12-inch skillet, heat oil over medium-high heat. Add shiitake and crimini mushrooms, and cook, stirring constantly, for 5 minutes, or until lightly browned. Turn off heat, add enoki mushrooms, and sprinkle with soy sauce.
3. Toss three quarters of mushroom mixture with sushi rice and scallions, and arrange on 4 plates. Garnish plates with remaining mushrooms and watercress sprigs.

Vegetarian *with* Egg

THESE RECIPES FORM THEIR OWN GROUP because there are many vegetarians who do not eat eggs. All are made with the traditional sweet omelet, *tamago,* and are joined by a colorful cornucopia of vegetables.

CARROT, ASPARAGUS, *and TAMAGO FUTOMAKI*

PREP: **25** MINUTES
BOIL: **4** MINUTES

MAKES 3 ROLLS (24 PIECES)

3 strips (⅓ inch) *tamago* (page 21)
1 medium carrot, peeled and cut into ¼-inch batons
6 thin fresh asparagus spears, woody ends discarded
3 sheets *nori*
3 cups seasoned sushi rice (page 18)
Wasabi to taste

1. Make *tamago*.

2. In a 2-quart saucepan, bring salted water to a boil over high heat. Add carrot, and boil for 3 minutes. Add asparagus, and boil for 1 minute more. Drain vegetables and plunge them into ice water to stop the cooking action. Drain again, and pat dry with paper towels.

3. To make rolls, treat each sheet of *nori* with 1 cup seasoned rice, and spread *wasabi* on top of rice. Place 1 strip of *tamago* and 2 asparagus spears on each sheet along with one-third of carrot pieces on top of rice and roll according to the method on page 35.

MIXED VEGETABLE *and* TAMAGO CHIRASHI-ZUSHI

PREP: **25** MINUTES
BOIL: **1½** MINUTES

MAKES **4** SERVINGS

2 cups diced *tamago* (page 21)
8 thin fresh asparagus spears, woody stems discarded and cut into 1½-inch pieces
24 snow peas, stemmed
4 cups seasoned sushi rice (page 18)
1 medium carrot, peeled and cut into julienne
1 cup *daikon* sprouts, rinsed
12 cherry tomatoes, halved

1. Make *tamago*.

2. In a 2-quart saucepan, bring salted water to a boil over high heat. Add asparagus, and boil for 1 minute. Add snow peas, and boil for 30 seconds more. Drain vegetables and plunge them into ice water to stop the cooking action. Drain again, pat dry with paper towels, and separate them by type.

3. Place rice in an even layer in serving bowl. Arrange asparagus, snow peas, carrots, sprouts, cherry tomatoes, and *tamago* on top in separate sections.

Raw Fish

RAW FISH IS SO JOINED WITH THE CONCEPT OF SUSHI that many people erroneously believe that sushi means fish rather than vinegared rice. These recipes are grouped by which fish is dominant, although there can also be supporting players. Feel free to experiment and swap fish as you please.

FRIED SALMON SKIN, SALMON, *and* SNOW PEA *FUTOMAKI*

PREP: **20** MINUTES
COOK: **7** MINUTES

MAKES **3** ROLLS (**24** PIECES)

SALMON SKIN
2 (8-ounce) thin salmon fillets
Freshly ground black pepper to taste
¼ cup all-purpose flour
2 cups vegetable oil

ROLL
16 snow peas
3 sheets *nori*
3 cups seasoned sushi rice (page 18)
Wasabi to taste

1. Rinse salmon fillets and pat dry with paper towels. Remove skin from fillets with a sharp knife, leaving ¼ inch of flesh attached to skin. Season skin with pepper, and dust with flour, shaking off any excess. Cut remaining raw salmon into ½-inch strips across the grain, and set aside.

2. In a 10-inch skillet, heat oil over medium-high heat. Add 1 skin and fry, turning it once with tongs, for 3 minutes, or until crisp. Drain fried skin on paper towels, and repeat with second skin. Cut each skin into 3 strips.

3. Cut snow peas in half lengthwise, and steam for 1 minute, or until bright green. Plunge snow peas into ice water to stop the cooking action; drain and pat dry with paper towels.

4. To make rolls, treat each sheet of *nori* with 1 cup seasoned rice, and spread *wasabi* on top of rice. Place 2 fried salmon skin strips, 2 slices salmon, and one-third of snow peas on top of rice and roll according to the method on page 35.

Note: The traditional way to prepare this dish is to broil the skin rather than fry it. I prefer it fried for its textural contrast, but either approach can be used.

SALMON-STUFFED TOFU POUCHES

PREP: **25** MINUTES

MAKES **12** PIECES

12 triangles seasoned *abura-age* (page 24)
½ pound salmon fillet, skinned
Wasabi to taste

½ cup finely diced cucumber
3 cups seasoned sushi rice (page 18)

1. Season *abura-age.*
2. Rinse salmon and pat dry with paper towels; go over salmon and remove bones with tweezers or a vegetable peeler. Cut salmon into ⅓-inch dice, and season with *wasabi* to taste.
3. In a medium bowl, combine salmon, cucumber, and rice. Mix gently with your fingers to combine, being careful not to break the rice.
4. Pull apart triangles, and loosely stuff with rice mixture.

SALMON *and* *TOBIKO* OMELET PURSES

PREP: 25 MINUTES
COOK: 10 MINUTES

MAKES **12** PIECES

OMELET
1 tablespoon cornstarch
2 tablespoons *mirin*
3 large eggs
3 large egg yolks
Pinch salt
1 tablespoon vegetable oil

PURSES
½ cup seasoned sushi rice (page 18)
½ pound salmon fillet, finely chopped
4 tablespoons *tobiko*
12 chives

1. In a medium bowl, stir cornstarch into *mirin* until it dissolves. Add eggs, egg yolks, and salt to bowl, and whisk well.
2. In a 12-inch skillet, heat oil over medium heat. Add half of egg mixture, and cook until egg sets. Turn gently with a spatula, and cook other side briefly. Place omelet on paper towels, and repeat with remaining egg mixture.
3. Cut each omelet into 6 circles 3 inches in diameter; set aside. Gently combine rice and salmon in bowl, and divide mixture among the 12 circles so that the lighter side of the omelet will be showing. Top filling with 1 teaspoon *tobiko*.
4. To form purses, pull up sides of circle around filling and tie purse closed with chive.

TUNA, SALMON, CRAB, *and* CUCUMBER *URAMAKI*

PREP: **15** MINUTES

MAKES 3 ROLLS (24 PIECES)

3 ounces tuna
3 ounces salmon
3 sheets *nori*
3 cups seasoned sushi rice (page 18)
Wasabi to taste
1 Japanese or Kirby cucumber or ¼ English cucumber, cut into ¼-inch batons
½ cup lump crabmeat
3 tablespoons *tobiko* for garnish, optional

1. Rinse tuna and salmon, and pat dry with paper towels. Cut both fish into ¼-inch strips.
2. To make rolls, treat each sheet of *nori* with 1 cup seasoned rice, and reverse onto plastic-covered bamboo mat.
3. Spread *wasabi* on top of nori, and divide tuna, salmon, cucumber, and crabmeat onto the 3 sheets. Roll according to the method on page 36, and garnish outside of rolls with *tobiko,* if using.

RICE PAPER PANCAKE *with* TUNA *and* ROASTED RED BELL PEPPER

PREP: **20** MINUTES
BROIL: **5** MINUTES

MAKES 4 ROLLS (8 PIECES)

1 large red bell pepper
½ pound tuna
Wasabi to taste
2 cups seasoned sushi rice (page 18)
3 tablespoons granulated sugar
4 rice paper pancakes

1. Preheat an oven broiler. Place red pepper on the rack of a broiler pan and broil 4 inches from broiler element until skin is charred and black, about 5 minutes, turning peppers with tongs to char all sides. Plunge pepper into ice water, and when cool enough to handle remove and discard cap, skin, and seeds. Cut pepper into ½-inch dice, and set aside.
2. Rinse tuna, and pat dry with paper towels. Cut tuna into ½-inch dice. Rub tuna cubes with *wasabi*.
3. Combine tuna, roasted pepper, and sushi rice in a bowl, and stir gently to combine.

3. Fill a wide mixing bowl with very hot tap water, and stir in sugar. Place a damp tea towel in front of you on the counter. Place rice paper pancakes on a plate, and cover with a barely damp towel.

4. Fill 1 rice paper pancake at a time, keeping remainder covered. Totally immerse pancake in hot water for 2 seconds. Remove, and place it on the damp tea towel; it will become pliable within a few seconds. Gently fold front edge of the pancake one-third of the way to the top. Place a quarter of filling on the folded-up portion, and shape it into a log, leaving a 2-inch margin on each side. Fold the sides over the filling, and roll tightly but gently, beginning with the filled side. Continue to fill rice paper pancakes in the same manner. Cut each roll in half.

YELLOWTAIL, MANGO, JICAMA, *and* ASPARAGUS *TEMAKI*

PREP: **15** MINUTES
COOK: 1½ MINUTES

MAKES **8** ROLLS

12 thin fresh asparagus spears, woody ends discarded
½ pound yellowtail
Wasabi to taste
¼ pound fresh jicama, peeled
4 sheets *nori*, cut in half
4 cups seasoned sushi rice (page 18)
1 small mango, peeled and thinly sliced

1. In a 2-quart saucepan, bring salted water to a boil over high heat. Add asparagus, and boil for 1½ minutes. Drain asparagus, and plunge it into ice water to stop the cooking action. Pat dry with paper towels, and cut into 4-inch lengths.

2. Rinse yellowtail, and pat dry with paper towels. Cut yellowtail into ½-inch batons that are 4 inches long; season with *wasabi*. Cut jicama into ¼-inch batons that are 4 inches long.

3. For rolls, treat each half sheet of *nori* with ½ cup seasoned rice. Divide up asparagus, yellowtail, jicama, and mango onto rice, and roll according to the method on page 37.

SPICY YELLOWTAIL *HOSOMAKI*

PREP: **10** MINUTES

MAKES **3** ROLLS (**24** PIECES)

¼ pound yellowtail
1 tablespoon mayonnaise
2 teaspoons chili paste
1½ sheets *nori*
1½ cups seasoned sushi rice (page 18)
Wasabi to taste

1. Cut yellowtail into 3 long strips. In a small bowl, stir together mayonnaise and chili paste. Rub mixture on yellowtail.

2. To make rolls, cut whole sheet of *nori* in half. Treat each sheet of *nori* with ½ cup seasoned rice, and spread *wasabi* on top of rice. Place yellowtail on top of rice and roll according to the method on page 34.

MIXED FISH *CHIRASHI-ZUSHI*

PREP: **15** MINUTES

MAKES **4** TO **6** SERVINGS

4 cups seasoned sushi rice (page 18)
¼ pound thinly sliced salmon
¼ pound thinly sliced yellowtail
¼ pound thinly sliced tuna
¼ pound thinly sliced barbecued eel
1 cup shredded *daikon*
½ cup shredded carrot
⅓ cup salmon roe
Shiso leaves for garnish, optional
Lemon slices for garnish, optional

Spread rice in an even layer in serving bowl. Arrange salmon, yellowtail, tuna, eel, *daikon*, carrot, and salmon roe on top in separate sections. Garnish with *shiso* leaves and lemon slices, if using.

SALMON, SOLE, CARROT, CUCUMBER, *and TAMAGO CHIRASHI-ZUSHI*

PREP: **15** MINUTES

MAKES **4** SERVINGS

1½ cups diced *tamago*
⅓ pound salmon fillet, skinned
⅓ pound thick sole fillet
1 large carrot, peeled and thinly sliced
1 Japanese or Kirby cucumber, thinly sliced, or ¼ English cucumber, cut into
   quarters lengthwise and thinly sliced
3 cups seasoned sushi rice (page 18)

1. Make *tamago.*
2. Rinse salmon and sole, and pat dry with paper towels. Remove any bones from fish with tweezers or a vegetable peeler. Dice fish into ⅓-inch pieces.
3. Mix three-quarters of fish, carrot, cucumber, and *tamago* with rice. Divide mixture onto 4 plates, and garnish top of plates with remaining ingredients.

Cooked Fish

WHILE TRUE AFICIONADOS RAISE EYEBROWS at the thought of using cooked fish as part of sushi, it is always a good idea at a sushi party to include at least one cooked dish. Don't think of cooked as boring—the whole world of smoked fish qualifies, and adds its salty lustiness to the mix of flavors and textures.

BARBECUED EEL *with* CARROT *and TAMAGO URAMAKI*

PREP: **25** MINUTES
COOK: **3** MINUTES

MAKES **3** ROLLS (**24** PIECES)

3 (⅓-inch wide) strips *tamago*
1 medium carrot, peeled and cut into ¼ inch batons
3 sheets *nori*
3 cups seasoned sushi rice (page 18)
Wasabi to taste
¼ pound barbecued eel fillet, cut into 3 strips
3 tablespoons black sesame seeds or toasted white sesame seeds (page 25) for
   garnish, optional

1. Make *tamago.*

2. In a 2-quart saucepan, bring salted water to a boil over high heat. Add carrot strips, and boil for 3 minutes. Drain carrot strips and plunge them into ice water to stop the cooking action. Drain again, and pat dry with paper towels.

3. To make rolls, treat each sheet of *nori* with 1 cup seasoned rice, and reverse onto plastic-covered bamboo mat.

4. Spread *wasabi* on top of *nori,* and place 1 barbecued eel portion and 1 *tamago*

strip on top. Divide carrots among the 3 rolls, and roll according to the method on page 36. Coat top of each roll with sesame seeds, if using.

SMOKED SALMON, PAPAYA, *and* AVOCADO *URAMAKI*

PREP: **15** MINUTES

MAKES **3** ROLLS (**24** PIECES)

¼ pound smoked salmon
3 sheets *nori*
3 cups seasoned sushi rice (page 18)
Wasabi to taste
1 ripe avocado, thinly sliced
½ small papaya, peeled, seeded, and thinly sliced
3 tablespoons *tobiko* for garnish, optional

1. Stack smoked salmon slices, trimming and pasting as necessary until they become a rectangle. Cut the rectangle into 3 long strips.

2. To make rolls, treat each sheet of *nori* with 1 cup seasoned rice, and reverse onto plastic-covered bamboo mat.

3. Spread *wasabi* on top of nori, and place 1 smoked salmon portion on top. Divide avocado and papaya among the 3 rolls, and roll according to the method on page 36. Coat top of each roll with *tobiko,* if using.

Shellfish

MOLLUSKS—EITHER RAW OR COOKED—and cooked crustaceans are some of my favorite forms of seafood. Their flavor is inherently sweet and delicate, and these qualities are enhanced by the seasoned sushi rice.

OYSTER *GUNKAN-ZUSHI*

PREP: **15** MINUTES

MAKES **24** PIECES

⅓ cup cocktail sauce
1 tablespoon *wasabi*
2½ cups seasoned sushi rice (page 18)
5 sheets *nori*
24 small shucked oysters, well drained
24 thin lemon slices for garnish (optional)

1. In a small bowl, stir cocktail sauce and *wasabi* together until well blended. Set aside.
2. Form *gunkan-zushi* according to the method given on page 32. Spoon 1 teaspoon cocktail sauce onto each, and top with 1 oyster. Place a lemon slice at one end of oval, if using.
   Note: Small shucked littleneck clams can be substituted for the oysters.

CALIFORNIA ROLL

PREP: **15** MINUTES

MAKES **3** ROLLS (**36** PIECES)

3 sheets *nori*
3 cups seasoned sushi rice (page 18)
Wasabi to taste
1 Japanese or Kirby cucumber or ¼ English cucumber, cut into ¼-inch batons
1 ripe avocado, thinly sliced
6 crab sticks or ¼ pound lump crabmeat

1. To make rolls, treat each sheet of *nori* with 1 cup seasoned rice, and reverse onto plastic-covered bamboo mat.

2. Spread *wasabi* on top of *nori*, and divide cucumber and avocado onto the 3 rolls. Place 2 crab sticks on each roll, and roll according to the method on page 36.

SHRIMP TEMPURA *HOSOMAKI*

PREP: **25** MINUTES PLUS **30** MINUTES CHILLING
FRY: **3** MINUTES

MAKES **24** PIECES

SHRIMP
Tempura Batter (page 22)
12 extra-large (16 to 20 per pound) raw shrimp
6 bamboo skewers
3 cups vegetable oil
½ cup all-purpose flour

ROLL
3 sheets *nori*
3 cups seasoned sushi rice (page 18)
Wasabi to taste

1. Make *Tempura* Batter and chill it for 30 minutes.
2. Peel and devein shrimp, leaving on last section of tail. Thread shrimp onto skewers to keep them straight, placing 2 per skewer.
3. In a 10-inch skillet with high sides or a saucepan, heat oil to a temperature of 375°F over medium-high heat. Dip shrimp

into flour, shaking off any excess, and then into *tempura* batter; fry for 2 to 3 minutes, or until browned. Remove shrimp from oil with tongs, and drain on paper towels. Remove skewers, and set shrimp aside.

4. To make rolls, cut each sheet of *nori* in half. Trim *nori* to size, if necessary, so that 2 shrimp meet in the middle with their tails extending out from the *nori*. Remove shrimp from *nori*. Then treat each sheet of *nori* with ½ cup seasoned rice, and spread *wasabi* on top of rice. Place shrimp on top of rice and roll according to the method on page 34.

5. Cut each roll in half at the point where the 2 shrimp abut, and then cut in half again. Serve pieces so tails extend upward on half of pieces.

Contemporary Concepts

WITH A FEW LIBERTIES TAKEN, all the recipes up to this point fall on the authentic side of the spectrum, but all of that is about to change. These recipes include a Mexican dish and some good old American favorites, too.

GUACAMOLE *and* SHRIMP *GUNKAN-ZUSHI*

PREP: **20** MINUTES

MAKES **24** PIECES

GUACAMOLE
2 ripe avocados
3 scallions, trimmed and chopped
1 jalapeño or serrano chile, seeds and ribs removed, and finely chopped
¼ cup chopped fresh cilantro
2 tablespoons fresh lime juice
Salt to taste

SUSHI
2½ cups seasoned sushi rice (page 18)
5 sheets *nori*
1 cup small cooked salad shrimp
24 thin cucumber slices for garnish (optional)

1. In a large bowl, mash avocado with scallions, chile, cilantro, and lime juice until smooth. Season with salt, and press a sheet of plastic wrap directly into the surface to prevent discoloration. Refrigerate for up to 6 hours.

2. Form *gunkan-zushi* according to the method given on page 32. Spoon guacamole onto each, and top guacamole with shrimp. Place cucumber slices at one end of oval, if using.

GRILLED SHRIMP, BASIL, *and* ASPARAGUS ROLLS

PREP: **20** MINUTES PLUS **2** HOURS MARINATING
COOK: **6** MINUTES

MAKES **3** ROLLS (**24** PIECES)

SHRIMP
6 (8-inch) bamboo skewers
12 large (21 to 25 per pound) shrimp
2 tablespoons olive oil
2 tablespoons dry white wine
1 garlic clove, peeled and crushed
1 teaspoon herbes de Provence or Italian seasoning
Salt and freshly ground black pepper to taste

ROLL
6 thin fresh asparagus spears, woody ends discarded
1/2 cup firmly packed fresh basil leaves
3 sheets *nori*
3 cups seasoned sushi rice (page 18)

1. Soak skewers in cold water. Peel and devein shrimp, then rinse and pat dry with paper towels.

2. In a 1-quart heavy resealable plastic bag, combine oil, wine, garlic, herbes de Provence, salt, and pepper. Mix well, and add shrimp. Marinate for 2 hours, refrigerated, turning bag a few times to marinate evenly.

3. Preheat a grill or oven broiler. Drain bamboo skewers and thread 2 shrimp on each skewer in a position to keep them straight. Grill shrimp for 2 minutes per side or until pink.

4. Steam asparagus for 1 to 2 minutes, depending on thickness. Plunge asparagus into ice water to stop the cooking action, then drain and pat dry with paper towels. Wrap each asparagus spear tightly with basil leaves.

5. To make rolls, treat each sheet of *nori* with 1 cup seasoned rice, and invert onto a bamboo mat covered with plastic wrap. Place 4 shrimp and 2 asparagus spears on nori, and roll according to the method on page 36.

SMOKED SALMON "SUSHI" *with* ASPARAGUS *and* SCALLIONS

PREP: **20** MINUTES
COOK: **2** MINUTES

MAKES 4 ROLLS (24 PIECES)

12 thin fresh asparagus spears, woody ends discarded
¼ pound mild goat cheese, softened
2 tablespoons light cream
2 teaspoons *wasabi* powder or to taste
8 large slices (½ pound) smoked salmon
1⅓ cups seasoned sushi rice (page 18)
4 scallions, green tops only

1. Steam asparagus for 1 to 2 minutes, depending on thickness. Plunge asparagus into ice water to stop the cooking action, then drain and pat dry with paper towels.
2. In a small bowl, combine goat cheese, cream, and *wasabi*. Stir well.
3. Arrange 2 salmon slices on a bamboo mat covered with plastic wrap. Spread one-quarter of goat cheese mixture on top of salmon.
4. Spread ⅓ cup rice on salmon, leaving ½ inch of edge uncovered. Place 3 asparagus spears and green tops from 1 scallion in center of rice, and roll according to the method given on page 35.

CHICKEN TERIYAKI *FUTOMAKI with* SCALLIONS

PREP: **15** MINUTES PLUS **4** HOURS MARINATING
BROIL: **8** MINUTES

MAKES 3 ROLLS (24 PIECES)

CHICKEN
1 (4-ounce) boneless, skinless chicken breast half
½ cup soy sauce
2 tablespoons *mirin*
1 tablespoon firmly packed light brown sugar
1 tablespoon toasted sesame oil
2 garlic cloves, peeled and crushed
2 teaspoons grated fresh ginger

ROLL
9 scallions, green parts only
3 sheets *nori*
3 cups seasoned sushi rice (page 18)

1. Rinse chicken and pat dry with paper towels. Trim off all visible fat, and place between 2 sheets of plastic wrap. Pound chicken with the flat side of a meat mallet or the bottom of a small heavy skillet to an even thickness of ½ inch.

2. In a 1-quart heavy resealable plastic bag, combine soy sauce, *mirin*, brown sugar, oil, garlic, and ginger. Mix well, and add chicken. Marinate for 4 hours, refrigerated, turning bag a few times to marinate evenly.

3. Preheat an oven broiler or grill. Remove chicken from marinade, and discard marinade. Grill chicken for 4 minutes per side or until chicken is cooked through and no longer pink. Allow chicken to cool, and cut it into 6 strips.

4. To make rolls, cut scallion greens to fit width of *nori*. Assemble rice, chicken, and scallions according to the method on page 35.

BLT *FUTOMAKI*

PREP: 15 MINUTES
COOK: 7 MINUTES

MAKES 3 ROLLS (24 PIECES)

6 strips bacon
⅓ cup mayonnaise
1 tablespoon *wasabi*
6 leaves romaine lettuce
3 ripe plum tomatoes
3 sheets *nori*
3 cups seasoned sushi rice (page 18)

1. In a large heavy skillet, cook bacon over medium-high heat until crisp. Remove bacon from pan, drain on paper towels, and set aside.

2. In a small bowl, stir together mayonnaise and *wasabi;* set aside. Cut thick rib out of each lettuce leaf. Discard core and cut each tomato in half lengthwise. Squeeze seeds out, and slice each half into ¼-inch slices.

3. To make rolls, treat each sheet of nori with 1 cup seasoned rice; spread one-third of mayonnaise mixture on top of rice. Place 2 bacon strips, 2 lettuce ribs, and one-third of tomato slices on top of rice and roll according to the method on page 35.

Five SMALL TOUCHES

T he recipes in this chapter are ones that round out a sushi party. They include some soups, vegetable pickles, and clearly nontraditional "dessert sushi." These foods are not the main event; the recipes for all different types of sushi are found in Chapter 4. But these dishes are fun to add to an event, and all are very easy to make.

Soups

IN TRADITIONAL JAPANESE RESTAURANTS soup is not served as a separate course; it arrives with the rest of the food. When I make sushi at home, however, I do serve the soup as a light appetizer, which adds a more leisurely pace to the dinner. Japanese soups are very light; they perk the palate without being too filling. And they are served in very small portions of about ½ cup, so if you want to be more generous, these recipes will feed 4 rather than 6.

MISO SOUP *with* TOFU *and* GREENS

PREP: **20** MINUTES
COOK: **5** MINUTES

MAKES **6** SERVINGS

3 cups *Dashi* Number Two (page 24)
2 tablespoons light *miso* paste
¼ pound firm tofu, cut into ½-inch dice
2 cups firmly packed bok choy greens, cut into ½-inch slices, optional
3 scallions, trimmed and thinly sliced

1. Make *Dashi* Number Two.
2. In a 2-quart saucepan, heat *dashi* until almost boiling over medium-high heat. Whisk ½ cup stock into *miso* paste, and then pour mixture back into saucepan.
3. Add tofu and greens, if using, to mixture, and bring to a boil over medium-high heat. Simmer 2 minutes or until greens are wilted. Serve immediately, garnished with scallion rings.
   Note: The bok choy is not an authentic part of this soup, but I find that it adds visual interest.

CLEAR SOUP *with* SHIITAKE MUSHROOMS *and* BEAN SPROUTS

PREP: **20** MINUTES
COOK: **6** MINUTES

MAKES **6** SERVINGS

3 cups *Dashi* Number One (page 23)
3 ounces fresh shiitake mushrooms
1 tablespoon soy sauce
1 tablespoon *sake*
¼ cup fresh mung bean sprouts, rinsed
2 scallions, trimmed and thinly sliced

1. Make *Dashi* Number One.
2. Rinse mushrooms, discard stems, and slice thinly.
3. In a 2-quart saucepan, heat *dashi,* soy sauce, and *sake* over medium-high heat until it comes to a boil. Add mushrooms, and simmer over medium heat for 3 minutes. Add bean sprouts, and turn off heat. Serve, garnished with scallion rings.

Pickles

WHILE THE VEGETABLES USED TO CREATE THESE PICKLES are part of Japanese cuisine, I find most authentic pickles rather boring; they are merely pickled in a combination of rice vinegar and sugar. So I have taken some liberties with these recipes and have included other ingredients. These pickles are not meant to be served in place of pickled ginger; these colorful and flavorful additions to a sushi meal should be served for nibbling.

RED ONION PICKLES

PREP: **10** MINUTES PLUS CHILLING
COOK: **10** MINUTES

MAKES **10** SERVINGS

1 pound small red onions
3 garlic cloves, peeled and halved
¾ cup rice vinegar
⅓ cup granulated sugar
1 tablespoon grated orange zest
1 teaspoon kosher salt
¼ teaspoon dried red chile flakes

1. Peel onions, cut them in half, and slice each half into ¼-inch rings. Set aside.

2. In a 2-quart nonreactive saucepan, combine garlic, vinegar, sugar, orange zest, salt, and chile flakes. Bring to a boil over medium heat, stirring occasionally to dissolve the sugar. Reduce heat to low and simmer for 3 minutes.

3. Add onions, and simmer for 4 to 5 minutes over medium heat, or until onions are soft. Remove and discard garlic cloves.

4. Transfer onions and liquid to a storage container, and cool to room temperature. Refrigerate for up to 1 week, and serve onions chilled.

GINGERED CARROT PICKLES

PREP: **15** MINUTES PLUS CHILLING
COOK: **10** MINUTES

MAKES **10** SERVINGS

1 pound thick carrots, peeled
¼ cup shredded fresh ginger
2 small serrano chiles, seeds and ribs removed, halved
1½ cups rice vinegar
⅓ cup firmly packed light brown sugar
1 teaspoon kosher salt

1. Cut carrots on the diagonal into slices 1/16 inch thick. Set aside.

2. In a 2-quart nonreactive saucepan, combine ginger, chiles, vinegar, sugar, and salt. Bring to a boil over medium heat, stirring occasionally to dissolve the sugar. Reduce heat to low, and simmer for 5 minutes.

3. Add carrots, and simmer for 3 to 4 minutes, or until carrots are crisp-tender. Remove and discard chiles.

4. Transfer carrots and liquid to a storage container, and cool to room temperature. Refrigerate for up to 1 week, and serve carrots chilled.

LOTUS ROOT PICKLES

PREP: **15** MINUTES PLUS CHILLING
COOK: **15** MINUTES

MAKES **10** SERVINGS

2 cups rice vinegar
1 pound fresh lotus root
²⁄₃ cup granulated sugar
1 tablespoon grated lemon zest
1 teaspoon kosher salt
¹⁄₂ teaspoon freshly ground white pepper

Lotus Root Pickles,
Gingered Carrot Pickles,
and Red Onion Pickles

1. In a large bowl, combine ¼ cup vinegar with 1 quart cold water. Bring a large pot of water to a boil.

2. Peel lotus root, and cut into rounds ¹⁄₁₆ inch thick, placing cut slices in acidulated water to prevent discoloration. Drain lotus root, and boil for 7 to 10 minutes or until slices are cooked but still slightly crunchy. Drain, and plunge slices into ice water to stop the cooking action. Place lotus root slices into a storage container.

3. While lotus root is boiling, combine remaining vinegar, sugar, lemon zest, salt, and pepper in a 2-quart nonreactive saucepan. Bring to a boil over medium heat, stirring occasionally to dissolve sugar. Simmer 2 minutes.

4. Pour liquid over lotus root, and cool to room temperature. Refrigerate for at least 2 days before serving, and then use within 1 week. Serve lotus root chilled.

Dessert Sushi

THERE IS NO AUTHENTIC WAY TO END A SUSHI MEAL on a sweet note; desserts as we know them in Western cuisines do not exist in Japanese cooking. What many fine sushi restaurants around the country do is serve fusion desserts by incorporating Asian ingredients like crystallized ginger or plum wine into French prototypes. But I decided to push this envelope a bit further for *Sushi with Style* with these recipes for dessert sushi. As is the case with their savory counterparts, once you have mastered making the rice, the forms are easy to replicate and open to endless variation.

For serving, use caramel sauce or chocolate sauce in your soy sauce dish, and any nut butter or thick fruit jam can become the stand-in for your dollop of *wasabi*.

RICE *for* DESSERT SUSHI

PREP: 5 MINUTES

MAKES 2 CUPS

2 cups hot cooked rice, unseasoned (page 17)
⅓ cup cream of coconut (Note: This is a sweetened product usually found in the
    same section as Bloody Mary mix and other drink bases; it should not be
    confused with coconut milk)
2 tablespoons rum or clear liqueur of your choice (such as Triple Sec, Kirsch,
    white crème de menthe, or white crème de cacao)

1. Cook rice using one of the methods described in Chapter 2.

2. Place rice in a medium bowl; do not use the wooden tub used for savory rice. Stir cream of coconut and rum together, and sprinkle over rice.

3. Use the paddle in an up-and-down cutting motion to spread the rice into a thin even layer; do not stir the rice to avoid breaking the grains. After the rice is spread into an even layer, turn over small portions gently to allow steam to escape. Keep turning rice until steam stops rising.

4. To keep the rice ready to use for up to 6 hours, wring out a clean lint-free dish towel, and completely cover the mixing bowl.

Forming Dessert Fingers (Nigiri-zushi): A supple slice of fruit takes the place of the savory toppings. Use either of the methods on pages 30 and 31 to make the fingers, using a small amount of jam on the fruit in place of *wasabi*. Fruits to use: slices of strawberries, kiwi, mango, pineapple, peach, or apricot. Use a thick jam of either the same flavor or a complementary flavor.

Forming Dessert "Battleship" Sushi (*Gunkan-zushi*): As is true with the savory counterparts, the collar on these fingers contains tiny or thin fillings. In the case of dessert sushi, form the bands from dried fruit leathers of your choice; they are sold in the whole foods area of supermarkets, health food stores, and Middle Eastern markets. Then rub the top of the rice with thick fruit jam. Suggested toppings: any chopped fruit, fresh raspberries or small blueberries, or miniature chocolate chips. Suggested garnishes: fresh mint leaves or a sprinkling of sweetened coconut.

Forming Dessert Scattered Sushi (*Chirashi-zushi*): As with the savory bowls, these can have all the fruits arranged on the top or mixed in. Use the rules on page 38-40 as a guide, and any fruits can be used.

CARAMEL SAUCE

PREP: **5** MINUTES
COOK: **10** MINUTES

MAKES 1½ CUPS

1½ cups granulated sugar
½ cup water
3 tablespoons unsalted butter
1 cup heavy cream
1 teaspoon pure vanilla extract

1. In a 1-quart saucepan, combine sugar and water, and bring to a boil over medium-high heat. Swirl pan by the handle but do not stir. Allow syrup to cook until it reaches a walnut-brown color, swirling the pot by the handle frequently.
2. Remove pan from the heat, and stir in butter and cream with a long-handled spoon; the mixture will bubble furiously at first. Return pan to low heat and stir until lumps have melted and sauce is smooth. Stir in vanilla, and transfer to a jar. Serve hot, room temperature, or cold; sauce can be refrigerated for up to 1 week.

CHOCOLATE SAUCE

PREP: 5 MINUTES
COOK: 6 MINUTES

MAKES 1½ CUPS

¾ cup water
½ cup granulated sugar
¼ cup light corn syrup
⅔ cup unsweetened cocoa powder
Pinch of salt
1 teaspoon pure vanilla extract

1. In a 1-quart saucepan, combine water, sugar, and corn syrup, and bring to a boil over medium heat, whisking until sugar dissolves.

2. Whisk in cocoa powder and salt, and reduce heat to low. Simmer for 3 minutes, then remove from heat, and stir in vanilla. Syrup can be refrigerated for up to 1 week.

Six DINING ON SUSHI

Now that you know how to make sushi, it is time to discuss the rituals that go along with eating sushi—both at home and at a restaurant. While there certainly are similarities between the two experiences, there also are differences. When dining at home the structure can be much less formal than that followed in a traditional sushi restaurant (*sushi-ya*).

Here is the great news: It is perfectly acceptable to eat sushi with your well-washed hands. So if you have been reticent to try eating, let alone making, sushi because you were afraid of embarrassment that your chopsticks would fly across the table, you are in luck. That is one less hurdle to jump.

The same is not true, however, for naked pieces of fish (*sashimi*) that are not propped up on rice cushions; they should always be transported from the plate with chopsticks. And it's common sense that bowls of scattered sushi (*chirashi-zushi*) should be eaten with chopsticks (or a fork).

Tips *for* All Occasions

IF YOU'RE USING CHOPSTICKS, DON'T RUB THEM TOGETHER or cross them on your plate. When not in use they should be placed parallel to each other either with their tips touching the chopstick rest (if you have one) or they can be placed across the top of the soy sauce dish.

Part of the fun of eating sushi is sharing, but never pick up a piece of food from another person's plate with the end of the chopsticks you put in your mouth. Use the thicker ends—the ones you hold—and deposit the food on your plate, and then turn the chopsticks around.

When passing food to another person, always offer the whole plate and not a single piece passed with your chopsticks. To the Japanese this is too reminiscent of the passing of a deceased relative's bones at a funeral, and for the same reason don't stick your chopsticks into the middle of the rice bowl; this vertical thrust is too close to incense sticks at a funeral. The final rule of group etiquette is a common sense covenant true of all meals eaten out. You never eat directly from a shared dish; always move some of the food to your personal plate with the thick ends of your chopsticks first.

While some restaurants in the United States make proper sushi eating a problem by a propensity for "super-sizing," all *nigiri-zushi* and pieces of *maki-zushi* should be eaten in a single bite after dipping the topping (*neta*) or *nori*, but *not* the rice into the soy sauce dish. It is considered very bad form to have grains of rice floating in your soy sauce saucer. If a piece of sushi is too large to eat in one bite, feel free to eat it in two, but don't set it back down on your plate once you have taken the first bite; it is considered very rude.

Also considered bad form, especially in restaurants, is stirring *wasabi* into the soy sauce dish. Chefs season sushi with the amount of fiery flavor they deem proper, and if you want more, rub some on the sushi itself.

The other traditional condiment, pickled ginger (*gari*), is supposed to be eaten between pieces of sushi as a palate cleanser. It is never eaten piled on top of the sushi itself, nor is it eaten as a random snack.

If you are enjoying alcoholic beverages, and you are in a group, it is considered polite to serve each other rather than pour your own drinks, and drinks are only refilled once the glass is empty. So in the true spirit of the Golden Rule, watch your fellow diners' glasses and they will do the same for you. And if you are toasting with an alcoholic beverage, the traditional Japanese toast is *kampai!*, which means "empty your cup." But you do not have to do it in one gulp!

Becoming *a* Champ *with* Chopsticks

WHILE EATING PIECES OF SUSHI WITH YOUR FINGERS IS FINE, learning how to properly maneuver chopsticks is useful so you can feel comfortable with all Asian cuisines. It helps if you think of them as a pair of tongs and your hand serves as the hinge with one stick held firmly and the other one moved up and down. There is no one definitive way to hold the chopsticks. As long as you can comfortably pick up the food and bring it to your mouth, you are using the chopsticks correctly.

Pick up the first chopstick with the middle finger and thumb. Stiffen your hand for a firm grip. Have the broad end of the chopstick lay on the part where your thumb and index finger connect. Rest the narrow end on the tip of your ring finger, and hold it in place with the tip of your middle finger. This part is constant, but there are a few alternatives for making the chopsticks work.

The first method is to grip the second chopstick with your index finger. Place your thumb over the second chopstick. Adjust your grip to a more comfortable position. Make sure the narrow tips of the chopsticks are even with each other to help prevent them from crossing or being unable to "pinch" the food. Hold it steady. This chopstick should not move when you attempt to pick up food.

Alternatively, hold the first chopstick steady and move the second (top) chopstick by moving the tip of your index finger up and down while the thumb remains relatively steady, acting like a pivot point. The top chopstick remains pressed to the index finger from the tip through the first joint. The movement comes from flexing the joint closest to the knuckle. Straightening your index finger opens the chopsticks and bending it closes them, with perhaps a slight flexing of the thumb to keep the chopsticks lined up with each other.

Practice opening and closing the chopsticks. Make sure the broad ends of the chopsticks do not make an X, as this will make it difficult to pick up food. Pick up food at a good angle (try roughly 45 degrees from the plate); lift it up a few inches. If it feels unstable, put it down and try again. Apply a firm but gentle pressure on the food, just enough to keep the food from falling from the chopsticks. Too much pressure is more likely to cause your chopsticks to cross at the narrow ends unless they're perfectly aligned and could launch your food across the table.

Watching Asian people eat can help you master this process, but start by using "training wheels." Asians will hold their chopsticks very far up toward the thick ends, but they are easier to control if you hold them closer to the thin end. And practice is the key to success, so if you're really interested in learning, use chopsticks at home when eating any small bits of foods, too.

When Dining Out

IF GREETED BY A JAPANESE HOST OR HOSTESS, chances are you'll hear *irasshaimase* (ir-ash-ay-mah-say), which means "please come in." If you're alone, or you want to watch sushi being made and have some interaction with the sushi chef (*itamae*), then ask to be seated at the bar; otherwise ask for a table. In either location the meal most likely will begin with the presentation of a hot wet towel (*oshibori*) to use on your hands only, and not your face or neck. Then fold it up neatly before returning it.

If you're sitting at the bar, do not treat the *itamae* as your server; all drinks, soup, and other non-sushi items should be ordered from real servers, although the *itamae* will be expecting to receive your food order. And do not be surprised if he never writes anything down but at the end of the meal the bill is perfect; keeping track of customers' tallies is part of their training. Servers should be addressed with the phrase *sumimasen* (su-mee-mah-sen), which is saying "excuse me" or "pardon."

True sushi aficionados rarely consult a menu; they order *omakase*, which literally means "to entrust" but in reality means "chef's whims." It is like the tasting menu in a Western restaurant; it can be a special experience for the brave, but it's not for everyone. Many skilled *itamae* will create elaborate presentations for *omakase* meals, and many *omakase* meals are not priced in advance on a menu, so if your budget is tight it might not be a comfortable alternative to traditional ordering.

Don't feel, however, that you are hostage once the request has been made. There are certain ways to direct the *itamae* without marring the spirit of the event. You can say "*omakase* but not *ebi*" if you're allergic to shrimp, or request that no *sashimi* be part of the plate.

While not necessary, it will endear you to the *itamae* if you offer him a beer or carafe of sake, especially if you've been asking a lot of questions. At the end of the meal thank the *itamae* with the phrase "*arigato gozaimasu*," (ah-ree-gah-toh go-zah-mah-zoo), which means "thank you very much," and tip the *itamae* for the food portion of the bill, and the server for the remainder; if you're at a table, just tip as normal. Most sushi bars have a jar for tips because the chef will not handle money while handling food. And if you are paying by credit card, it's possible to split the tip as you would between the captain and the waiter in a Western restaurant.

One change from Western restaurants is that all the food arrives at the table at once; there is no such thing as courses. If you are not given a spoon with your soup, do not ask for one. Lift the bowl to your mouth with both hands, and sip the broth. When the bowl is empty, eat the solids with your chopsticks. And regardless of what you are eating in a Japanese restaurant, the "clean plate club" from your childhood rules; it is considered impolite to not finish your food, and even lower on the manners scale is to pick some ingredients out of a slice of *maki* and leave others.

Serving Sushi *at* Home

ONCE YOU HAVE MASTERED EVEN A FEW FORMS OF SUSHI, you probably will want to share your creations with friends. Hosting a sushi party is a fun and relaxing way to entertain.

As is the case with any party, start by planning your menu and work schedule. For the menu, compile a list of ingredients that provide enough variety to suit your guests' food tastes. It is a good idea to make sure you have at least one totally vegetarian item, and select a few dishes that contain cooked seafood rather than raw.

Begin with the time you want the first pieces to be delivered to the table, and then back-time each element you must accomplish so you can determine when you should begin working; it is always a good idea to factor in some extra time to reduce your stress. Include such tasks as setting the table and straightening the kitchen before guests arrive.

When making sushi, always begin with the vegetarian items because they are less perishable than those that contain raw fish or cooked seafood. However, you can prep the raw fish and seafood hours in advance and keep it refrigerated, covered with plastic wrap.

The second consideration when planning the cooking schedule for a sushi party is the use of *nori*; it starts out crisp but quickly turns soggy. While all forms of *maki* rolls can withstand the sogginess for a few hours without falling apart, especially inside-out rolls, which are really held together by the rice, it is not a good idea to complete hand rolls in advance.

Part of the fun of hosting a sushi party is creating your stage set; this is not the time for Grandma's starched white linens, best china, and polished sterling flatware. Imagine your house is a sushi restaurant, and try to find simple props that convey a Zen minimalist approach. Bamboo or straw placemats can be found at many discount stores; they form the base of all table settings.

The proper way to set each place setting is with the chopsticks parallel to the bottom edge of the table with the chopstick rest on the left; even if people are left-handed the chopsticks are set this way. Above the chopsticks is the soy sauce dish, once again placed on the left, and whatever beverage glass is being used is placed on the right side of the plate. Rather than setting a large dinner plate, I usually use salad plates for each person; the plate is only used for a few pieces of sushi at a time and a larger plate makes the individual bites look lonely!

I find that for a centerpiece a single spray of cymbidium orchids or even a few tall thin leaves are the most effective, except in spring when a low bowl of peonies remind me of traditional Japanese screen paintings. Another approach is to float a single flower in a bowl of water, perhaps with some floating candles. In lieu of flowers, you can also try a low bowl of colored glass marbles.

There is no need to purchase the rectangular plates used in sushi restaurants to create attractive serving platters. This is where your dinner plates come in handy; with garnishes they are the perfect size for an 8-piece *maki* roll. During the summer I clip hosta leaves from my garden to decorate the plates, and then add whatever herb flowers or nasturtiums are in bloom. During the winter any colorful green can serve the same function; Swiss chard, leaf lettuce, or the large white-veined leaves from bok choy are all attractive. For pretty vegetable garnishes for your sushi platters, see the ideas in Chapter 2.

When serving sushi, remember that the magic number is five. You can serve fewer, or you can serve more pieces, but *never* six. That is the number associated with death. Traditionally just one form of sushi is served on a plate, but when I have a large group sitting at the table I will do two or three identical platters with a few different types to keep passing to a minimum.

In your own home the pace of a meal can be more leisurely than at a sushi bar at which everything is delivered simultaneously. I serve soup first, and then possibly a green salad, before starting with the sushi. And, as you've seen with the recipes in Chapter 4, you can carry the sushi theme through to dessert.

Beverages

WHAT TO DRINK WITH SUSHI IS A SUBJECT OPEN TO MUCH DEBATE. The real consideration is that the beverage should not overwhelm the delicacy of the food; even with a smear of *wasabi* here and there, sushi has clear and bright flavors that are not softened by fat like a French cream sauce.

While *sake* is always associated with Japanese cuisine, technically it is not supposed to be poured with sushi because they are both rice based; it is usually reserved for *sashimi.* But in this country that rule is often ignored.

Sake is very much like wine; it ranges in flavor greatly from sweet to dry, and those produced by high-end manufacturers have a complex flavor that balances fruit flavors and acidity. In some ways it is a cross between beer and wine; it is closer to beer because it is made from a grain rather than a fruit, yet it contains the same alcoholic content as wine (usually between 12 percent and 18 percent), and it comes in a number of styles. Here are the main styles:

Junmai-shu is purely fermented rice with no added alcohol. It has a rich flavor and pairs well with almost all Japanese food, including sushi.

Honjozo-shu is similar to *junmai-shu* but does have a small percentage of added alcohol. I consider this a great choice for serving warm.

Ginjo-shu is lighter in body that the previous two because the rice is milled so that only about half of the grain remains. It has a delicate fragrance.

Daiginjo-shu is the lightest body on the scale, and is made with the most refined wine.

Historically *sake* was served warm both because it developed centuries before refrigeration, and also because the higher temperature masked certain imperfections in its flavor. Today, however, the choice is up to you. To heat the *sake,* pour it into a ceramic or glass carafe (*tokkuri*) and place it in a pan of boiling water; the water should extend halfway up the sides of the carafe. Turn off the heat, and allow the carafe to sit for 3 to 5 minutes. Test the temperature of *sake* the way you would for a baby's bath. Sprinkle some on the underside of your wrist; it should be warm but not hot.

In the Japanese tradition, and especially during the day, green tea is what purists drink, and never with the addition of milk or any sort of sweetener. It is now easy to find high-quality green tea in almost all supermarkets because it is deemed a powerful antioxidant.

Tea should be brewed in small batches, and it *never* should be allowed to sit on the leaves after its brewing time. Place 2 tablespoons of tea leaves in a ceramic pot that has been rinsed out with very hot water. Then add 3 cups boiling water, and stir gently. Allow the tea to steep for 1 minute, and then strain it into the tea pot from which it will be served. You can use the leaves a second time for another pot.

Beer and wine are becoming more popular as beverage choices for sushi. In Japan beer is the country's most popular drink; it accounted for two thirds of alcohol sales in 2006. In general, Japanese beers are light in character; they were introduced to the country by German and Dutch traders. The most popular brands exported are Kirin, Sapporo, and Asahi, and you can find them almost everywhere.

Serving wine with sushi presents a challenge, and that is because of the *wasabi* sauce. I have found you cannot go wrong with Champagne or any good-quality sparkling wine. The effervescence and yeasty notes serve as a foil to the richness of some fish, and the body is light.

Crisp and dry white still wines also pair well. Stay away from the buttery and oaky California Chardonnays in favor of Sancerre, Savignon Blanc, and Chablis. White Bordeaux is an excellent match with most sushi, as is a Pinot Blanc.

But red wine lovers need not be left out, as long as the red is not too high in tannins. Pinot Noirs from either Burgundy or the United States are excellent with some of the "meatier" fish like tuna, and Beaujolais is another choice that blends well.

Glossary

THERE ARE MYRIAD JAPANESE WORDS SPRINKLED about in the text of this book—this list will help you to understand them and pronounce them. Note: No syllable of a Japanese word is emphasized more than another.

abura-age (ah-boo-rah-ah-geh)—Fried tofu pouches that are cooked and then stuffed with sushi rice.

aemono (ah-eh-moh-noh)—Vegetables (or sometimes meats) mixed with a dressing or sauce.

agari (ah-gah-ree)—Green tea, as it's called in sushi bars.

agemono (ah-geh-moh-noh)—Foods that are either pan-fried or deep-fried.

aji (ah-jee)—Spanish mackerel.

aka miso (ah-ka-mee-soh)—Red soybean paste.

akagai (ah-ka-gah-ee)—Red clam.

akami (ah-kah-me)—Lean cut of tuna.

anago (ah-nah-goh)—Saltwater eel precooked and grilled before serving.

anko (ahn-koh)—Monkfish.

awabi (ah-wah-bee)—Abalone.

biiru (bee-roo)—Beer.

buri (boo-ree)—Adult yellowtail.

buta (boo-ta)—Pork.

chirashi-zushi (chee-ra-shee-zoo-shee)—Scattered sushi, with ingredients arranged on top of rice or mixed into rice.

chutoro (choo-toh-roh)—The upper belly area of a tuna; not as fatty as *otoro*.

daikon (dah-ee-kohn)—A giant long white radish.

dashi (dah-shee)—Basic soup and cooking stock usually made from *kombu* (kelp) and *katsuo-bushi* (dried bonito flakes).

ebi (eh-bee)—Shrimp when they are served cooked.

edamame (eh-dah-mah-meh)—Young green soybeans served cooked.

futomaki (foo-toh-mah-kee)—Thick rolls.

gari (gah-ree)—Pickled ginger.

gobo (goh-boh)—Long, slender burdock root.

gohan (goh-hahn)—Plain boiled rice.

goma (goh-mah)—Sesame seeds.

gunkan-maki (goon-kahn-mah-kee)—Battleship roll with a collar of *nori* to hold in soft ingredients.

hamachi (hah-mah-chee)—Young yellowtail tuna.

hamaguri (hah-mah-goo-ree)—Hard-shell clam.

hanakatsuo (hah-nah-kah-tsoo-oh)—Dried bonito fish that's shaved or flaked.

hashi (hah-shee)—Chopsticks.

hijiki (hee-jee-kee)—Black seaweed in tiny threads.

hikari-mono (hee-kah-ree-mo-no)—Fish sliced for serving with the shiny silver skin still attached.

hirame (hee-rah-meh)—Halibut.

hocho (hoh-choh)—Cooking knives.

hosomaki-zushi (hoh-soh-mah-kee-zoo-shee)—Thin rolls.

hotategai (hoh-tah-teh-gah-ee)—Scallops.

ika (ee-kah)—Squid.

ikura (ee-koo-rah)—Salmon roe.

inada (ee-nah-dah)—Very young yellowtail.

inari-zushi (ee-nah-ree-zoo-shee)—*Abura-age* stuffed with sushi rice.

itamae (ee-tah-may)—Sushi chef.

kajiki (kah-jee-kee)—Swordfish or marlin.

kaki (kah-kee)—Oysters.

kani (kah-nee)—Crab meat, always served cooked.

kanpyo (kahn-piyoh)—Dried gourd strips.

kappa-maki (kah-pah-mah-kee)—Cucumber rolls.

karei (kah-reh-ee)—Flounder.

katsuo (kah-tsoo-oh)—Bonito.

katsuo-boshi (kah-tsoo-oh boo-shi)—Bonito flakes.

kazunoko (kah-zoo-noh-koh)—Herring roe.

kohada (koh-hah-dah)—Japanese shad.

kuro goma (koo-roh-goh-mah)—Black sesame seeds.

maguro (mah-goo-roh)—Tuna.

makisu (mah-kee-soo)—Bamboo mat in which *maki-zushi* is rolled.

maki-zushi (mah-kee-zoo-shee)—A roll made with rice and other ingredients wrapped in a sheet of *nori*.

masago (mah-sah-goh)—Smelt roe.

masu (mah-soo)—Trout.

matoudai (mah-toh-dai)—John Dory.

mirin (mee-rin)—Sweet rice wine for cooking.

mirugai (mee-roo-ghai)—Geoduck or horseneck clam.
miso (mee-soh)—Soybean paste.

moyashi (moh-yah-shee)—Bean sprouts.

nasu (nah-soo)—Eggplant.

negi (neh-gee)—Scallion or green onion.

neta (neh-tah)—The topping for a piece of *nigiri-zushi*.

nigiri-zushi (nee-ghee-ree-zoo-shee)—Fingers of rice topped with *wasabi* and another ingredient, most often raw seafood.

nori (noh-ree)—Sheets of dried seaweed used in making all forms of *maki*.

ocha (oh-chah)—Tea.

ohyo (oh-hyoh)—Halibut.

oshibori (oh-shee-boh-ree)—A hot towel offered before the meal.

oshi-zushi (oh-shee-zoo-shee)—Pressed sushi made in a wooden mold.

otoro (oh-toh-roh)—The fattiest portion of a tuna, found on the underside.

ponzu (pohn-zoo)—Sauce made with soy sauce and Japanese citron.

saba (sah-bah)—Mackerel, almost always served after being salted and pickled.

sake (sah-keh)—Rice wine, or salmon.

sashimi (sah-shee-mee)—Small slices of raw fish fillets served without rice.

shiitake (shee-tah-keh)—Japanese mushroom available dried or fresh.

shiro goma (shee-roh-goh-mah)—White sesame seeds.

shiro maguro (shee-roh mah-goo-roh)—White albacore tuna.

shiso (shee-soh)—Leaf of the perilla plant.

shoga (shoh-gah)—Fresh ginger root.

shoyu (shoh-yoo)—Japanese soy sauce.

soba (soh-bah)—Buckwheat noodles.

su (soo)—Rice vinegar.

suimono (soo-ee-moh-noh)—Clear soup.

suzuki (soo-zoo-kee)—Striped bass.

tai (tah-ee)—Red snapper or porgy.

tairagi (tah-ee-rah-gah-ee)—Razor shell clam.

tako (tah-koh)—Octopus.

tamago (tah-mah-goh)—Sweet egg omelet cooked in a square pan.

tekka-maki (tek-kah-mah-keh)—Tuna roll.

temaki-zushi (teh-mah-kee-zoo-shee)—Hand rolls with rice and other ingredients wrapped in a cone of *nori*.

temari-zushi (teh-mar-ee-zoo-shee)—*Nigiri-zushi* formed in plastic to a round ball shape.

tempura (tem-poo-rah)—Deep-fried batter-coated seafood or vegetables.

tobiko (toh-bee-koh)—Flying-fish roe.

tori (toh-ree)—Chicken.

torigai (toh-ree-gah-ee)—Japanese cockle.

toro (toh-roh)—Fatty tuna.

udon (oo-dohn)—Wide wheat noodles.

unagi (oo-nah-gee)—Freshwater eel.

uni (oo-nee)—Sea urchin.

uramaki-zushi (your-ah-mah-kee-zoo-shee)—Inside-out rolls.

usukuchi shoyu (oo-soo-koo-chee-shoh-yoo)—Light Japanese soy sauce.

wakame (wah-kah-meh)—Dried lobe-leaf seaweed in long, dark green strands.

wasabi (wah-sah-bee)—Japanese horseradish.

yakimono (yah-key-moh-noh)—Broiled foods.

Mail-Order Sources

THERE ARE FEW EXPERIENCES AS FRUSTRATING AS HAVING A MENU all planned, only to find your local supermarket is out of stock of a key ingredient. The good news is that the rudimentary supplies for making sushi are now carried nationally. You are likely to find better prices at an Asian grocery than the supermarket. Such staples as rice vinegar play a role in all Asian cuisines, so even if the grocery is Thai or Korean it is a good bet you will also find Japanese foods.

Finding some of the specialized equipment such as sushi molds or edibles like sushi-grade fish is more difficult. But you can let your cursor do the shopping. The list of Web sites is exhaustive, so I have narrowed it down to ones I have used and have been happy with both the quality of the product and their customer service.

Asian Food Grocer
131 West Harris Avenue
San Francisco, CA 94080
888-482-2742
www.asianfoodgrocer.com

Bemka Company
2801 SW 3rd Avenue, Suite F11A
Ft. Lauderdale, FL 33315
877-462-0533
www.caviarlover.com

Catalina Offshore Products Inc.
5202 Lovelock Street
San Diego, CA 92110
619-297-9797
www.catalinaop.com

Ethnic Grocer
1090 Industrial Drive, Suite 5
Bensenville, IL 60106
630-860-1733
www.ethnicgrocer.com

House of Rice Store
3221 N. Hayden Road
Scottsdale, AZ 85251
877-469-1718
www.houserice.com

Katagiri & Co.
224 East 59th Street
New York, NY 10022
212-755-3566
www.katagiri.com

Pacific Mercantile Company
1925 Lawrence Street
Denver, CO 80202
303-295-0293
www.pacificeastwest.com

Sushi Foods Co.
1620 National Avenue
San Diego, CA 92113
888-81-SUSHI
www.sushifoods.com

Metric Equivalents

THESE RECIPES USE THE STANDARD UNITED STATES method for measuring ingredients (teaspoons, tablespoons, and cups). The information on this chart is provided to help cooks outside the United States use these recipes. All equivalents are approximate.

EQUIVALENTS FOR LIQUID INGREDIENTS BY VOLUME

U.S.								Metric		
¼ tsp	=							1 ml		
½ tsp	=							2 ml		
1 tsp	=							5 ml		
3 tsp	=	1 tbls			=	½ fl oz	=	15 ml		
		2 tbls	=	⅛ cup	=	1 fl oz	=	30 ml		
		4 tbls	=	¼ cup	=	2 fl oz	=	60 ml		
		5⅓ tbls	=	⅓ cup	=	3 fl oz	=	80 ml		
		8 tbls	=	½ cup	=	4 fl oz	=	120 ml		
		10⅔ tbls	=	⅔ cup	=	5 fl oz	=	160 ml		
		12 tbls	=	¾ cup	=	6 fl oz	=	180 ml		
		16 tbls	=	1 cup	=	8 fl oz	=	240 ml		
		1 pt	=	2 cups	=	16 fl oz	=	480 ml		
		1 qt	=	4 cups	=	32 fl oz	=	960 ml		
						33 fl oz	=	1000 ml	=	1 liter

EQUIVALENTS FOR DRY INGREDIENTS BY WEIGHT

(To convert ounces to grams, multiply the number of ounces by 30.)

1 oz	=	1/16 lb	=	30 g
4 oz	=	¼ lb	=	120 g
8 oz	=	½ lb	=	240 g
12 oz	=	¾ lb	=	360 g
16 oz	=	1 lb	=	480 g

EQUIVALENTS FOR LENGTH

(To convert inches to centimeters, multiply the number of inches by 2.5.)

1 in	=					2.5 cm		
6 in	=	½ ft	=			15 cm		
12 in	=	1 ft	=			30 cm		
36 in	=	3 ft	=	1 yd	=	90 cm		
40 in	=					100 cm	=	1 m

EQUIVALENTS FOR COOKING/OVEN TEMPERATURES

(To convert Fahrenheit to Celsius, first subtract 32 from your Fahrenheit temperature. Multiply that result by 5/9 to get the equivalent Celsius temperature.)

	Fahrenheit	Celsius	Gas Mark
Freeze Water	32° F	0° C	
Room Temperature	68° F	20° C	
Boil Water	212° F	100° C	
Bake	325° F	160° C	3
	350° F	180° C	4
	375° F	190° C	5
	400° F	200° C	6
	425° F	220° C	7
	450° F	230° C	8
Broil			Grill

Index